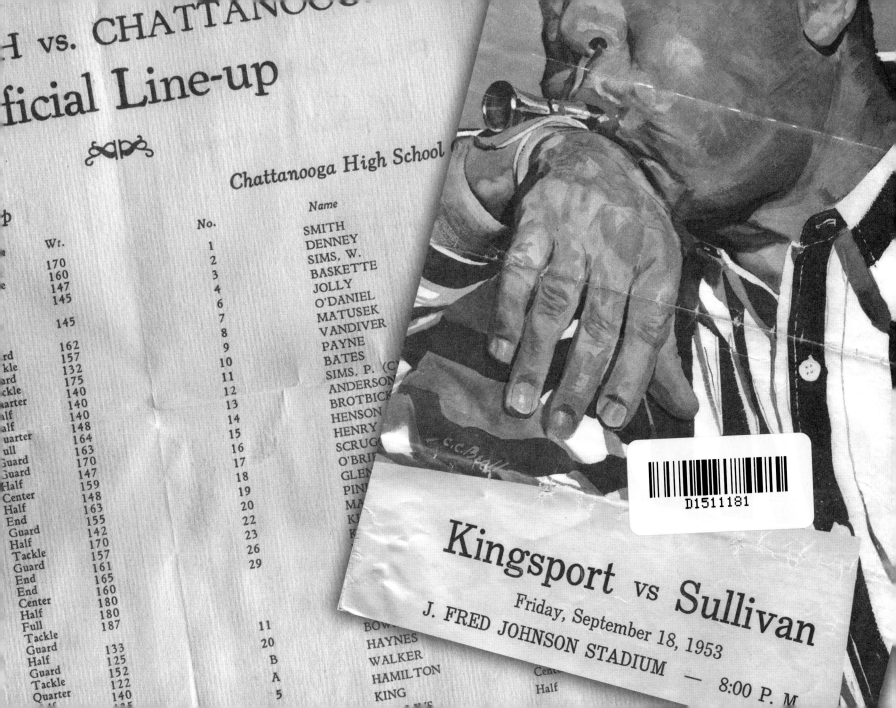

H vs. CHATTANOOG...

ficial Line-up

Chattanooga High School

	Wt.	No.	Name
	170	1	SMITH
	160	2	DENNEY
	147	3	SIMS, W.
	145	4	BASKETTE
		6	JOLLY
	145	7	O'DANIEL
		8	MATUSEK
rd	162	9	VANDIVER
kle	157	10	PAYNE
ard	132	11	BATES
ckle	175	12	SIMS, P. (C)
uarter	140	13	ANDERSON
alf	140	14	BROTBICK
alf	148	15	HENSON
uarter	164	16	HENRY
ull	163	17	SCRUG
Guard	170	18	O'BRI
Guard	147	19	GLEN
Half	159	20	PIN
Center	148	22	MA
Half	163	23	K
End	155	26	
Guard	142	29	
Half	170		
Tackle	157		
Guard	161		
End	165		
End	160		
Center	180		
Half	180		
Full	187		
Tackle		11	BOW
Guard	133	20	HAYNES
Half	125	B	WALKER
Guard	152	A	HAMILTON
Tackle	122	5	KING
Quarter	140		

c.c.B...

D1511181

Kingsport vs Sullivan

Friday, September 18, 1953

J. FRED JOHNSON STADIUM — 8:00 P. M

Game Time!

The Spirit of Sports in the Holston River Valleys

Published by

KINGSPORT TENNESSEE
TimesNews

From the Covers

Charity game

In 1950, the alumni of Shoemaker High School took on the Oklahoma Indians for a charity game. Among the former Shoemaker High School players on the team were Paul Whited (No. 7), Bernie Ervin (No. 9), and Sherman Warren (No. 2), a former All-American. Among the fans watching the game under the backboard were Loyd R. McClellan, Tommy Ramey, Betty Craft and Peggy Wolfe. The photo was taken by Herbert J. McClelland using a Crown Graphic 4x5 camera. McClelland was a war photographer during World War II and later sold sports photos to the Kingsport Times-News. Contributed by Herbert J. McClelland of Kingsport.

The team at Appalachia

The Appalachia High School football team played in a simple stadium behind the school in 1933. Among the players were Ralph Rotenberry (No. 16, back row, third from left), who played running back and later played at Emory & Henry College and at Virginia Tech; and Joseph E. "Bones" Scott (No. 30, front row, third from left). Contributed by David Rotenberry of Kingsport.

Preface

The swish of basketball through the net. The thud of football hitting the receiver's pads. The crack of bat making contact with baseball. The trumpets' blast mingles with tubas' oompah. The cheerleaders shout. The fans cheer. The sounds of sports echo through the years, resurrecting our memories of slim victories, new records, long-lasting friendships. In "Game Time! The Spirit of Sports in the Holston River Valleys" those memories get new life in photographs of teams and times past. From the turn of the 20th century through 1979, sports -- from baseball to basketball, football to golf, tennis to swimming -- have brought people together, engendering communities that supported and cheered their athletes on. Cheerleaders, bands and fans complete the picture of what these games have meant to the region. And now the time has come to relive those memories; it's "Game Time!"

Cheerleaders' chauffer

Chuck McClellan helped support the Church Hill High School cheerleaders by driving Wanda Jenkins (left), Chuck's then-girlfriend, now wife; and Rhenda Pierce, through Kingsport's Fourth of July Parade. Contributed by Chuck McClellan of Mount Carmel.

Acknowledgements

Game Time! *The Spirit of Sports in the Holston River Valleys*

Diana Meredith, *Project Director*

Becky Whitlock, *Book Editor*

Andrew Barnes, *Book Design and Production*

Bill Robinson, *Project Assistant*

Carroll Dale

Randy Wyatt

Pat Kenney

Bill Lane

Carmen Musick

Marci Gore

Kalee Nagel

Jeff Lambert

George Hutchins

Debbie Salyers

Keith Wilson, *Kingsport Times-News Publisher*

A special thank you goes out to all who have submitted photos for this unqiue sports history!

Miners at bat

Mining camps throughout Southwest Virginia fielded baseball teams for moments of recreation when they were away from their back-breaking work. In the first decade of the twentieth century, Milton Huff (back row, third from left) was among those miners. His father worked as the postmaster in Keokee, Virginia, so it is believed that Milton Huff worked in either Rawhide or Bundy, both mining towns. Contributed by Jerry Laningham of Church Hill.

Lettermen

The 1914 Bristol, Tennessee, High School football team wanted to show their toughness off the field as well as on. Their uniforms appear to offer only minimal protection. Contributed by Kenneth Depew of Kingsport.

Don't mess with this team

The Arcadia baseball team of 1912 was more than ready to play ball near Bloomingdale School. The team consisted of (front row, from left) Cliff Leonard, Joe Dunn, Bill Dunn, Rule Hicks, Dudley Hicks, Joe Pecktol, (back row, from left) Hassell Hicks, Melvin Richard Hickam, Sam Perry Fain, John Myers, A.F. Robinson, Joe Fain, Hicks Faulk and Harry Ketron. Contributed by Bill Hickam, grandson of Melvin Richard Hickam, of Kingsport.

Playing at Horse Creek

The Horse Creek School fielded a five-man basketball team in 1922, Alonzo Bayer (front row, holding ball), Ervin Ledbetter (front row, right), (back row, from left) Onnie Conkin, Kelly Ledbetter and Enoch Hood. Bill Jones (front row, left) was the school's principal and coach of the team, which played on an outdoor court with a simple wooden backboard. Horse Creek School is now Sullivan School. Contributed by Kenneth Depew of Kingsport.

Uniform team

The members of the Bristol, Tennessee, High School basketball team, circa 1910s, favored the longer shorts seen again on twenty-first century athletes. This team also seemed to like matching its socks to its sleeveless jerseys. Contributed by Grant Depew of Kingsport.

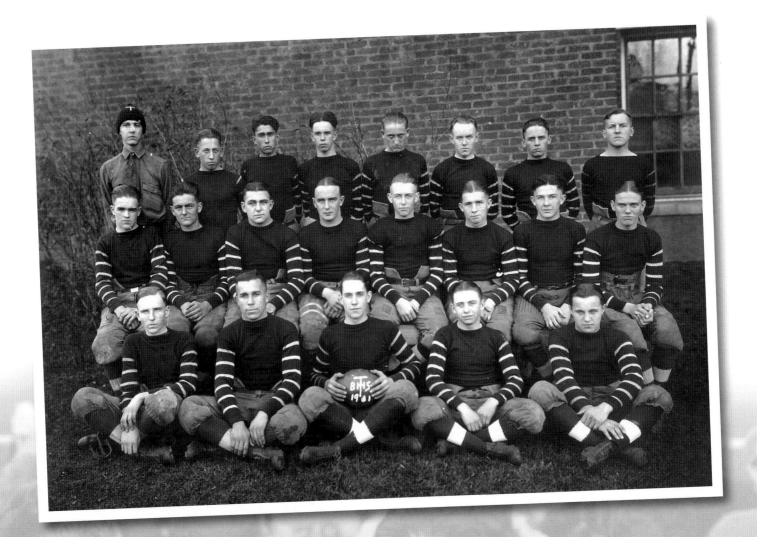

Tough and ready

The 1921 Bristol, Tennessee, High School football team appears more than ready for any opponent. Contributed by Grant Depew of Kingsport.

Ready to run

The 1920 Greeneville High School track team consisted of (front row, from left) Hal Hardin; Carl (last name unknown), captain and coach; Molly Lawsons, (second row, from left) Jay Barnett, Harry (last name unknown), Anna Belle (last name unknown), Tee Kirk, unknown, Paul Smith and Billy Harmon. Contributed by Grant Depew of Kingsport.

Tackle at ease

Broughton Hutchins, a future dentist in Kingsport, played tackle for Dobyns-Bennett High School from 1928 to 1931. Contributed by George Hutchins, son of Broughton Hutchins, of Kingsport.

Besting Kingsport

Prior to the 1937-38 basketball season, Blountville High School's Coach Elbert Humphreys tried to schedule a game against Dobyns-Bennett High School. D-B's then-Coach Leroy Sprankle turned Humphreys down for a regular-season game, saying he "did not desire to waste time with a team like Blountville," but offered to play a practice game on a Saturday morning. Humphreys declined the offer. However, the two teams did meet, during the state tournament in Lenoir City, Tenn., and Blountville beat the Kingsport school. The team members were (front row, from left) Coach Humphreys, Frank Wine, Harold Walton, unknown, Rex Shaver, (back row, from left) Lake Barnes, Bill King, G.C. "Jocko" Hays, York Feathers and unknown. Contributed by Earl Feathers, brother of York Feathers, of Kingsport.

It's in the genes

The Borden Mills baseball team won trophies for its season circa 1925. Andy Long (front row, second from left) was the team's catcher. His great-great-grandson is now the catcher for the Dobyns-Bennett High School baseball team. Contributed by Bill Long, grandson of Andy Long, of Kingsport.

District champions

The Rogersville High School girls' basketball team of 1932 were the 15th District champions. The team members were (from left) Gladys Horton Haynes, captain; Kate Kyle; Josephine Orr Miller; Ruth Doty Wheeler; Virginia Lyons Carson; Ann Webb Armstrong; Irene Wilson Kneale; Gladys Grigsby Cooper; Beatrice Price Miner; and Pauline Livesay Anderson. Gladys Horton married John Haynes, the quarterback of the Rogersville High School football team. Contributed by Susan Farrow, niece of Gladys Horton Haynes, of Rogersville.

Big win for Arcadia

The Arcadia baseball team won big -- 35 to zero -- in this game in the eastern part of Sullivan County. The 1937 team consisted of (seated on ground) Pete Faulk, (on bench, from left) John T. Hicks, J. Craft "Lefty" Akard, unknown, John N. Hicks, Boyd Hickam, Sam Hickam, Charlie Dixon, (standing, from left) unknown, unknown, W.F. Hicks, Price Hickam, Charlie Nottingham, Hiram Faulk and unknown. Maynard Faulk is the boy next to Pete Faulk. Contributed by Bill Hickam, son of Boyd Hickam, nephew of Sam Hickam and Charlie Notthingham, and related to Price Hickam, of Kingsport.

Winners by a point

During the 1935 basketball season, Dungannon High School girls' basketball team won the county championship over Hiltons High School by one point. The team members, most of whom were from Fort Blackmore, Virginia, were (front row, from left) Lillian Quillen Banner, Nola Horne Flanary, Magdalene Gibson Cassell, Myronelle Osborne Colley, Emily Brickey Johnson, Ina Johnson Martin, (back row, from left) Jo Taylor Cox, Lois Taylor Osborne, Blanche Flanary, Lakie Cox and Ardie Baldwin. Contributed by Valice Pierson, daughter of Nola Horne Flanary, of Gate City, Virginia.

Hold that line

The 1936 Dobyns-Bennett High School football team was a force to be reckoned with, racking up an 11-1 record that season. Among the team members were (from left) Oliver "Brud" Hawk, Jake Mosier, Metri Ballis, Dan McCaffey, Lawson Groseclose, Bobby Peters, Tom "Slats" Burgan, Bobby Cifers, Carl Downa, M.T. "Simp" Smith, Jim "Paddle" Blessing, L.M. "Coach" Rich and Hugh "Flash" Blessing. Contributed by Keith Hamilton (Chandler) Gregory and Bob Hawk, both of Kingsport.

Gate City's first

The year 1931 was the year high school football came to Gate City, Virginia. The school's first team consisted of (front row, from left) George Cox, tackle; Robert Munsey, guard; Arthur Stair, center; Hershel Catron, guard; Joe Catron, tackle; (middle row, from left) Bob Lilly, quarterback; Logan Flanary, quarterback; Dee Minnich, guard; Foxy Whited, guard; Kyle Davidson, tackle; (back row, from left) Ernest Quillen, coach; Ezra Carter, end; Luke Whited, fullback; Roy Compton, halfback; and Boford Snodgrass, end. In that first year, the team beat East Stone Gap, 6-0 and Haysi, 33-0, and tied Kingsport in its first game 0-0. However, it lost against Big Stone Gap, Kingsport (in the rematch), Clintwood and Pennington. The team's uniforms were hand-me-downs from Dobyns-Bennett High School, a transaction which Arthur Stair's father, the supervisor of Scott County Schools, was able to arrange. Several of the boys spent an "extra" year in school because they knew football would begin in 1931. Contributed by Majorie Stair of Kingsport.

Brothers play baseball

Eleven of the sixteen Bowen brothers from Duffield, Virginia, were well-known throughout the region in the 1930s for their baseball playing. The Bowens played the Duncans of Kingsport, which also fielded a team of brothers, in August 1935 and in 1936. Also in 1936, the Bowens played the Blatz brothers of Ohio at the General Motors annual picnic in Dayton, Ohio, and a minor league team in Marion, Virginia. The Bowens lost all four games, but enjoyed playing baseball nonetheless. The team circa 1939 consisted of (front row, from left) Jake, Harmon, (back row, from left) Emmitt, Clarence, Minner, Jay, Fred, Porter, Slemp, Tom and Coy. Contributed by Bill Bowen, younger brother of the Bowens, of Kingsport.

Hawkins County champs

The Church Hill Elementary School basketball team won the Hawkins County championship in 1939. The team members, who were in seventh and eighth grades, were (front row, from left) Bill Pangle, Paul Bradshaw, Johnny Taylor, Jack Pratt, H.M. Collins, (second row, from left) W.B. Christian, Dick Wallace and Rice Sams. Johnny Taylor, 13 and in the eighth grade, was captain of the team, and he and W.B. Christian were named All-County, an honor awarded by the county's coaches and referees. Johnny Taylor and Dick Wallace are the only two team members who are still alive. Contributed by Marsha Cox, daughter of Johnny Taylor, of Kingsport.

Blocked punt

In 1938, during the first playoff game in the history of the East Tennessee title race, Dobyns-Bennett High School versus Chattanooga Central, Oliver "Brud" Hawk, center for D-B, blocked Chattanooga's punt in the last three minutes of play, picked up the ball and ran it to the Chattanooga 12-yard line. On the next play, Bobby Cifers (not pictured) scored, and D-B won 13-12. Contributed by Kathy Hawk of Kingsport.

Great athlete

Bobby Cifers is the greatest documented athlete from the Holston River Valley region. He played for Dobyns-Bennett High School in the late 1930s and was the national high school scoring champion in 1938, the state scoring champion in 1939 and holds the record for the most Tennessee Secondary Schools Athletic Association first-place medals with 13. He is the all-time leading scorer at D-B with 491 points, and during his junior and senior years he was named to the first team for the All-State, All-Southern, All-Mid South and All-American teams. In addition to football, Cifers played basketball, and was captain of the basketball team. He also was undefeated as the pitcher for the baseball team. He later played football at the University of Tennessee and led the nation in Division I punting. During World War II, he served in the Army Air Corps. In 1946, he was the first-round draft pick by the Detroit Lions. He still holds the National Football League punting record for a minimum average of four punts per game at 61.8 yards. The photo is courtesy of Christopher and Kayley Cifers and was contributed by Tom Williams of Kingsport.

All-American

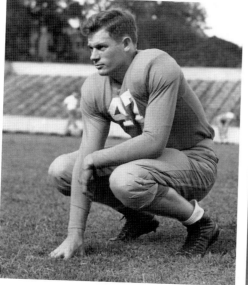

"Big" Ed Cifers played football for Dobyns-Bennett High School in the early 1930s and was the first player east of Knoxville recognized as an All-State player in 1933. He was a starter on the University of Tennessee football team under Coach Neyland. He played in the 1938 Sugar Bowl, the 1939 Orange Bowl and the 1940 Rose Bowl. In 1941, he was a first-round draft pick for the Washington Redskins, and he and fellow Redskin Sammy Baugh were the only first team All-Pro players off the 1942 world champion Redskins team. Cifers was Baugh's favorite receiver in that championship year. During World War II, Cifers served in the U.S. Navy, and he finished his football career playing for the Chicago Bears under the leadership of Coach George "Papa Bear" Halas. In 1965, Cifers was selected to Sports Illustrated's 25th anniversary All-American Team, the members of whom were selected by the impact they had on their fellowman. Among the honorees, besides Cifers, were Gerald Ford, Jackie Robinson and Mark Harmon, father of the actor. The photo is courtesy of the Leake, Pettit and Manning families, and was contributed by Tom Williams of Kingsport.

Kingsport's team

The professional baseball team in Kingsport in the late 1920s and early 1930s consisted of 15 men. The first names of many are no longer remembered. The team members were (kneeling, from left) Hobe Brummett, Roheleder, O'Rourke, Devins, Tevens, Harry Layne, Moody, (standing, from left) Herman Layne, Farley, McCabe, Kopshaw, Weldon, Wycalles, Cortney and Williams. The boy sitting in front is believed to be the son of O'Rourke. The photo is from the collection of Carl L. Cooper, the father of Jacquie Dishner of Blountville, who contributed it.

Star athlete

Carl E. "Short" Pettigrew, who, despite his nickname, stood six feet, six inches tall, was a star athlete for both Virginia High and Tennessee High schools, and in keeping with his athleticism, he was an accomplished dancer. In 1940, he played center for H.P. King Department Store in the Kingsport Industrial League. At the outbreak of World War II, he joined the U.S. Army, and died on April 11,1945, in Germany, as part of General George S. Patton's Third Army. Contributed by Pam Pettigrew Hutchins, daughter of Carl E. "Short" Pettigrew, of Kingsport.

Rocky Springs baseball

The Rocky Springs baseball team in the 1930s consisted of (front row, from left) Allison Spurgeon, Irby Ramsey, Oss Hicks, Herbert White, (second row, from left) Sam Ramsey, Dave Hicks, Lester Hamilton, (first name unknown) Jones and Clarence Dearstone. The Rocky Springs area is near Piney Flats. Contributed by Dwane Dishner, great-nephew of Allison Spurgeon, of Knoxville.

'Tiny' Blue Devil

James O. "Tiny" Roberts was an offensive lineman in 1949 for the Shoemaker High School Blue Devils, which played on Kane Field in Gate City, Virginia. Roberts played his entire high school career at Shoemaker. Contributed by Brent Roberts of Gate City, Virginia.

Busy season

Fairvew High School, in Scott County, Virginia, had a busy schedule during the 1946-47 season playing Clinchport, Fort Blackmore, Hiltons, Manville, Midway, Cleveland and Rye Cove high schools. The team members were (front row, from left) Jimmy Minor, Bruce Junior Bledsoe, Frank Jennings, (back row, from left) Maynard Joyner, Omar McMillon, Gilmer Bledsoe, Herb Michael, Errol Benton and Coach Omar Neely. At the time, the only gym in Scott County was the old Shoemaker gym in Gate City, so the county tournament was played there. Contributed by Jo Ann Roberts Bledsoe of Duffield, Virginia.

Football in wartime

In 1941, the Dobyns-Bennett High School football team lost some players to the draft in the days prior to the United States' entry into World War II. However, those who still were playing at the school, which at that time was located on Wateree Street, were (front row, from left) Bert Jacobs, Jack Crawford, Red Johnson, Coy Chambers, Alf Crawford, June Tranbarger, Sam Powell, (back row, from left) Howard Earles, Billy Harkins, Lawrence Mitchell and Hagan Bright. Only Billy Harkins and Hagan Bright are still living. The low building seen in the background of the photo was the field house. Contributed by W.Y. Harkins of Kingsport.

Scholarship athlete

Denver Crawford played on the Dobyns-Bennett High School footbal team in the early 1940s and earned a scholarship to play at the University of Tennessee, where he played all four years. Contributed by Pat Crawford of Kingsport.

Athletes to coaches

John Bell (left), Denver Crawford, Carl Jones and Beryl Shipley were involved in football, track and basketball in the 1940s at Dobyns-Bennett High School. All four, who got together for this photo at the Jan-Mar Restaurant in downtown Kingsport, later went on to coach sports at the high school or college level. Contributed by Pat Crawford of Kingsport.

Driving down the fairway

Ruby Webster Davis enjoyed playing golf in 1945 at the course that was once located in the Green Acres area off Eastman Road. Contributed by Opal Robertson, sister of Ruby Webster Davis, of Kingsport.

Coach Akard's team

The Sullivan High School basketball team of 1947 included Eldon Dykes (No. 3), Bobby Steadman (No. 5), Kenner Depew (No. 4) and Hal Morrison (No. 7). The managers were J.W. Blevins (standing, left) and H.L. Riggs (standing, second from right). Coach Akard (standing, right) was the coach. Contributed by Stan Depew of Kingsport.

First putt

Donald Robertson was already taking up golf in 1947 at 3 years of age. At 55, he was killed by a drunk driver. Contributed by Opal Webster Robertson, mother of Donald Robertson, of Kingsport.

Wise County champs

In 1946, Norton High School won the Wise County football championship. The team members were (first row, from left) Hank Hankins, Bill Gleason, Joe Mack Yeary, Leroy Lyons, John Bernhardt, Ligon Lovelace, Mark Hillman, Gene Cury, L.E. Quillen, (second row, from left) Jimmy Sturgill, Fred Van Bever, Reid Erwin, Jack Nard, David Ball, Harold Duncan, Joe Stump, George Cose, Carl McAfee, Bill Gobble, Ronald Teague, Don Flanary and A.J. Lawson. Contributed by Dr. Hank Hankins Jr., of Wise, Virginia.

Manville baseball

The 1946 Manville baseball team, which played in the Scott County, Virginia, league, consisted of (front row, from left) Tom Campbell, Pat Gilliam, Bob Joe Jennings, Joe Bill Webb, Orville Gilliam, Bill Gilliam, (back row, from left) Walter Carter, Hoyt Pendleton, Claude Ervin, Ford Hubble and Jim Gilliam. The bat boy was Ronnie Gilliam. Jim and Bill Gilliam were twin brothers; Jim was the pitcher and Bill was the catcher. Among the teams this group played were those from Nickelsville, Rye Cove and Dungannon. Contributed by Alice Gilliam Arnold, daughter of Jim Gilliam, of Kingsport.

Four years of basketball

Mary Depew played high school basketball all four of the years she attended Hiltons High School in Hiltons, Virginia. This photo is circa 1948-49. Contributed by Mary Depew of Mount Carmel.

Halls Restaurant team

Halls Restaurant sponsored a boys junior leage basketball team in 1949-50, which included (from left) Bodie Scott, Bill Green, unknown, Donnie Adams, unknown, Bob Rule, Stanley Still, Locke Carter and unknown. Contributed by Paul "Bodie" Scott of Kingsport.

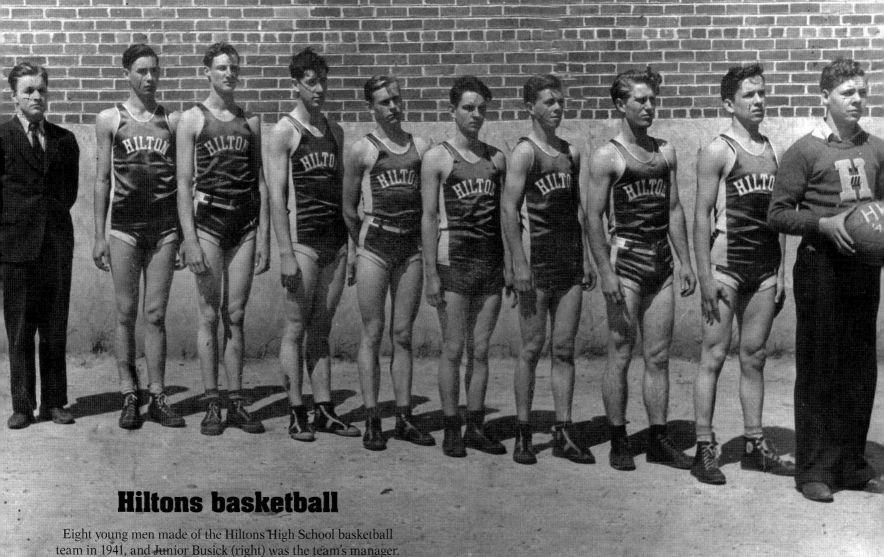

Hiltons basketball

Eight young men made of the Hiltons High School basketball team in 1941, and Junior Busick (right) was the team's manager. Contributed by Mary Depew of Mount Carmel.

Kingsport basketball

One of the inner-city basketball teams in Kingsport in circa 1948-49 consisted of (front row, from left) Tommy Barrett, Buddy Kerney, David Devault, Baldy Jones, (back row, from left) Red Elam, Buddy Bernard, Bill King, Lanny Fletcher and Buck Lane. Contributed by Phyllis Kerney of Kingsport.

First baseman

Glenn W. Haynes, a native of Moccasin Gap, now Weber City, Virginia, played first base with the Weber City Baseball Team in 1948 and 1949. Haynes' mother sewed the letters on his uniform, which he and his wife still have. Bill Compton was the team's manager. Haynes now lives in Kingsport. Contributed by Gladys Haynes of Kingsport.

Strike-out record holder

Dr. N.C. Russin played baseball for the UCLA Bruins from 1943-44 while serving in the U.S. Navy during World War II. He tied the college strike-out record by throwing 20 strikes. After the war, Russin moved to Kingsport and worked as a chemist at Eastman Kodak. While in Kingsport, he played baseball in leagues in Moccasin Gap and Gate City, Virginia. Contributed by Sally Russin Dingus of Blountville.

State champions

In 1947, Kingsport's Douglass High School won the state championship, the first and only it ever won. Among the players were Bobby Joe Johnson (left), Robert Graves and Jack Pierce. With only 20 players on the team, all the team members had to play both offense and defense, and no one could afford to get hurt. Robert Graves (deceased) later received a scholarship to play football at Morris Brown College in Atlanta. Contributed by Jack Pierce of Kingsport.

Lost Mountain player

After serving in the U.S. Navy during World War II, Billy Shanks returned to Northeast Tennessee and played baseball in 1946 for the Lost Mountain baseball team of Baileyton. He pitched and played left field. He later served as a baseball umpire for games at Sullivan West High School. Contributed by Pauline Shanks of Kingsport.

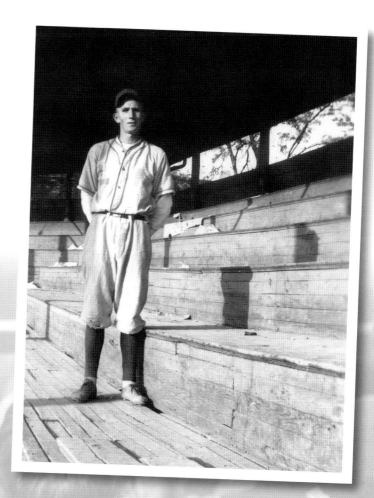

Championship team fullback

Thomas H. Howard was the fullback on Dobyns-Bennett High School's state championship team in 1946. Contributed by Kelly Jo Howard, daughter of Thomas H. Howard, of Kingsport.

Junior Industrial League champs

The winner of the Junior Industrial League in 1945-46 was a team sponsored by Moore & Walker insurance agency of Kingsport. The team members were (front row, from left) Ralph Burton (deceased), Carl Lucas, Edgar Helton, (back row, from left) J.T. McGrady (deceased), unknown, Bill Boggs and Joe Beard (deceased). Contributed by Joanne McGrady, wife of J.T. McGrady, of Kingsport.

Early years

Dorman Stout started playing baseball when he was just 7 or 8 years old in 1942-43, picking up bat and ball in front of his house. He passed on his love of baseball to his son Lamarr Stout, who played for the junior varsity team at John Sevier Junior High in 1974. Contributed by Mary Ann Stout of Kingsport.

Magnavox team

Magnavox sponsored a basketball team in the Greeneville Recreation League in Greene County in 1948. The team members consisted of (front row, from left) Olan Kilday, Cotton Craft, Phil Maupin, unknown, (second row, from left) Jack H. Kilday, Kyle Hawkins, unknown, (first name unknown) Livingston, and Onnie Kilday. Jack Kilday moved from Greeneville to Kingsport in 1950 and played fast-pitch softball for the Kingsport Press from 1950 to 1963, and won the Kingsport city league championship three years in a row. Jack Kilday, who served in and was wounded during World War II, is a cousin to Onnie and Olan Kilday. He and Kyle Hawkins also played baseball together. Contributed by Jack Kilday of Kingsport.

Ready to run

The Dobyns-Bennett High School track team in 1949 consisted of (from left) Jack Cox, Don Koth, Bob Morrow, Byron Wilburn, Orbin Taylor and Carlton Davis. Contributed by Shirley Taylor, wife of Orbin Taylor, of Kingsport.

City champions

The Dobyns Taylor basketball team won the 1947 Kingsport city championship. The team members were (front row, from left) Raymond Douglas Killian, ball boy; Lon V. Boyd; Fred L. Saylor; James M. Pendleton; (back row, from left) Emory A. Henry; Charles Harr; Usif Haney; Lawrence W. Thayer; Gentry W. Henry and coach Raymond Blair Killian. Contributed by Betsy Boyd, wife of Lon V. Boyd, of Kingsport.

In the minors

Charlie Heffner, who worked as an umpire for 45 years for high school and college games, played with the Kingsport Cherokees in the early 1940s. Charlie served in the U.S. Army and played on its baseball team, competing against major league teams. However, he found that at that time he could make more money playing in the Appalachian League than in the major leagues, because a collection was taken up from the fans at the minor league ball games. Heffner played every position, except pitcher and first base. Contributed by Jim and Janet (Heffner) Wells of Kingsport.

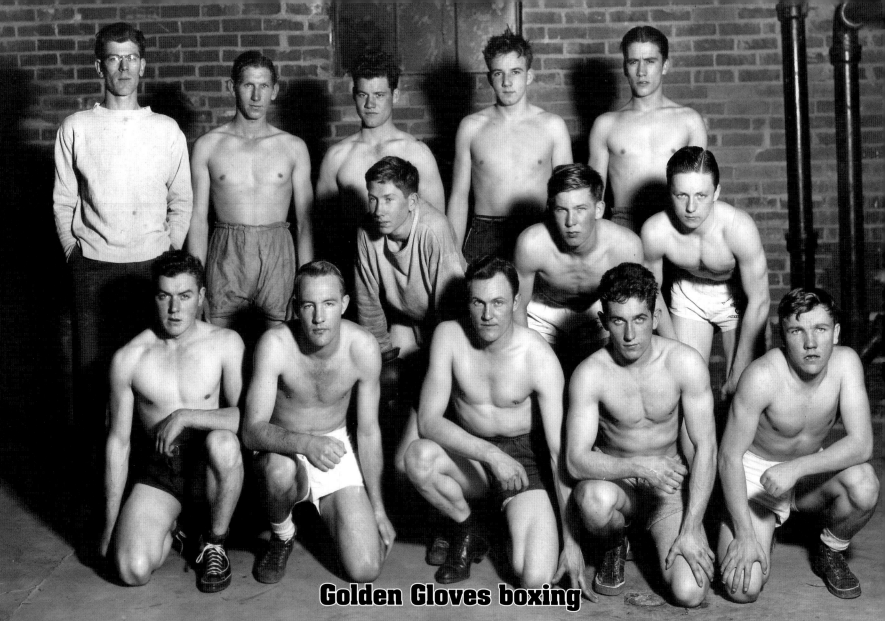

Golden Gloves boxing

The 1941 Kingsport Boxing Team participated in the Golden Gloves Tournament in Knoxville and won the team trophy. The team members were (front row, from left) Dick Dolen, H.C. "Duck" Dickson, Charlie Chandler, Ralph Price, Carson Glover, (middle row, from left) Ira D. Lane, Charles "Chuck" Taylor, Kenneth Jones, (back row, from left) Curtis S. Williams Jr., coach and manager; Clarence "Zip" Patrick; Felix O'Neal; Paul Pickens; and Jimmy Keith. The team, which Williams formed, broke up shortly thereafter and entered military service for World War II. Only Ira Lane and Ralph Price are living. Contributed by Ruth Williams, wife of Curtis S. Williams Jr., of Gray.

Sullivan County championships

The Lynn Garden Elementary School basketball team won the eighth-grade Sullivan County basketball championship in 1948-49. The team members are (front row, from left) Jim Fleming, Bob Morelock, Don Harkleroad, Bill Biggs, Dickie Warren, (back row, from left) Billy C. Dishner, Franklin "Red" Head, Ronald Hall, Clarence McMurray and Jack "Pete" Hauslee. Contributed by Carolyn Judd, niece of Ronald Hall, of Kingsport.

Shoemaker band

The Shoemaker High School Band was part of a parade down Main Street, now West Jackson Street, in Gate City, Virginia in 1948. Alfred Newton (deceased) was the drum major, and Roy Newton was the bass drummer. Roy Newton was in the band for two years and then he entered the U.S. Army to serve in the Korean War. Contributed by Roy Newton of Kingsport.

Junior high basketball

The members of the 1945-46 Kingsport Junior High basketball team were (front row, from left) Roy Cloud, Gary McGinnis, Gordon Blessing, Jerry Vaughn, Harvey Light, (second row, from left) Mr. S.O. Price, Pal Barger, Howard McCary, Johnny King, John Brown, Buddy Carter, Dr. Ellery Lay, (back row, from left) Bobby Page, manager; Ralph Mercer, Bob Morrow, Denver Cook, Tom Vaughn and June Kinny, manager. Contributed by Jean Blessing, wife of Gordon Blessing, of Kingsport.

Playing basketball

Lon V. Boyd played basketball at Dobyns-Bennett High School in the 1940s and received a basketball scholarship to play at Tusculum College, where he stayed for one year. He then attended East Tennessee State University, and played in several Kingsport city league teams. Contributed by Betsy Boyd, wife of Lon V. Boyd, of Kingsport.

The last two

Glen Fleenor and Bill King were Dobyns-Bennett High School's last two quarterbacks of the 1940s and each led the team to state championships in 1949 and 1950. King was a member of the class of 1949 and went on to play at the University of Virginia. Fleenor was a member of the class of 1950 and went on to play at Virginia Tech. Contributed by Jean Fincher of Kingsport.

D-B's starters

The starting infield of Dobyns-Bennett High School's 1949 baseball team were Bill King, Lee Crawford, Gary McGinnis and Glen Fleenor. They were coached by Guy B. Crawford (not pictured). Contributed by Jean Fincher of Kingsport.

Vertical leap

Bruce Wilder was a forward for the Dobyns-Bennett High School basketball team during his senior year in 1955. Contributed by Patti Wilder of Kingsport.

Drawing a crowd

Plenty of Lynn View High School football fans turned out at J. Fred Johnson Stadium to watch their team take on Dobyns-Bennett High School's football team in October 1957. Among the fans were Carl Marcum (second row, third from left), and Estelita McClain (fourth row, first one visible from left). Contributed by Donnie Jones of Gate City, Virginia.

Boxing buddies

Jake Sells (left), Buddie Russell and Wallace Ketron were members of the boxing team at the Kingsport Boys Club in the late 1950s. Buddie Russell, who was the assistant director and boxing coach with Charlie Pendleton at the Boys Club, was the seventh boy to join the Kingsport Boys Club, saying, "It was a godsend for me. It got me off the street." Russell later formed his own Russell Athletic Club on Long Island in the late 1950s and early 1960s and worked to racially integrate boxing in the region. Contributed by Buddie Russell of Surgoinsville.

Notable team

The 1955 Dobyns-Bennett High School varsity basketball team won the district that season and placed second in the regional and in the state tournaments. The team members were (front row, from left) Bruce Wilder, Bill Greene, Stan Johnson, Coach Guy B. Crawford, (second row, from left) Bill Britts, Charlie Leonard, Carl Bell, Al Warren, (third row, from left) Jim Taylor, Howard Johnson, Ronald White, Chuck Ross, David Lionberger and Coach Robert DeVault. Charlie Leonard later went on to play professional baseball, and Bill Greene founded and serves as chairman of BancTenn Corp., the parent company of Bank of Tennessee, and is chairman of Carter County Bank. Contributed by Bruce Wilder of Kingsport.

Watch the ball

James Crigger played football for Lynn View High School in
1956. Contributed by James Crigger of Mount Carmel.

Basketball practice

James Crigger played basketball for Lynn View High School in 1956.
Contributed by Janet Crigger of Mount Carmel.

Indian tradition

The Dobyns-Bennett High School band included an Indian chief and an Indian princess, who in 1950 was portrayed by Jackie Miller Depew. Contributed by Stan Depew of Kingsport.

All-Stars

The 1955 Kingsport Babe Ruth All-Star team consisted of (front row, from left) Vernon Lott; Dave Mullins; Tom Addington; Lynn Johnson; Mike Haulsee; Roy Harmon, manager; Robert Leonard, bat boy; Mike O'Neill; (second row, from left) Billy Amos; Wayne Harrell; Ron Scott; Jerry Richardson; Ron McConnell; Mel Joseph; Bob Strickler; Charlie Leonard; Jerry Murrell; Charlie Pennington, coach; and Hal McHorris. The players came from different Babe Ruth teams sponsored by Dobyns Taylor, the Boys Club, the Kingsport Elks and the Lions. Contributed by Charlie Leonard of Jonesborough.

First state championship

In 1953-54, the Nickelsville High School basketball team brought home the Group III state championship for the first time in Scott County's history. The team consisted of (from left) Coach Glen Addington (deceased), James Francisco, Wayland Isaacs, Paul Robinson (deceased), Ronald Dougherty, Bobby George, H.K. Dean, Paul George and Gary Vicars. Contributed by Jewell George of Kingsport.

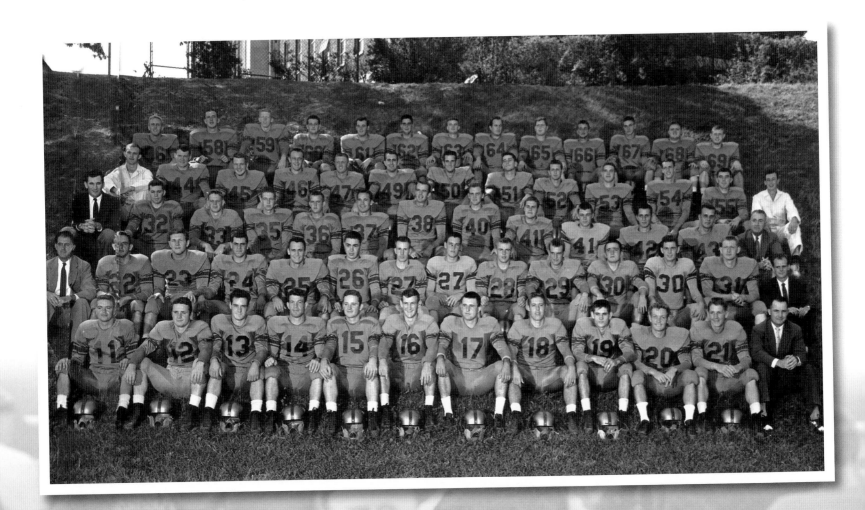

Bucs football

The 1954 East Tennessee State College Buccaneers football team had 58 players, including No. 23 Wallace Ketron (second row, third from left).
Contributed by Wallace and Nina Ketron of Kingsport.

Band officers

The band officers for the Church Hill High School band in 1958 were (from right) Jim Walter, Nina Arnold, Ferris Erwin, Janie Stroupe and Carolyn Jackson. Zane Gray was the band director. Contributed by Nina Ketron of Kingsport.

First drum major

Shelby Wells Christian was the first drum major of the Church Hill High School band and, in 1955, was given the chance to wear the band's first uniforms. From the collection of Lee H. and Mabel Marshall Stroupe.

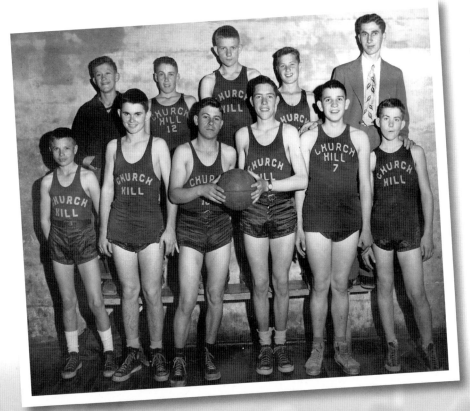

Two years of football

Jackie Barker played football at Lynn Garden Elementary School in 1955 and then played for one year at Lynn View High School in 1956. He and his wife, the former Charlotte Barrett, a Lynn Garden and Lynn View alumna, and their family now live in South Carolina. Contributed by Pauline Barker, mother of Jackie Barker, of Kingsport.

Enjoying basketball

The 1953 Church Hill Elementary School seventh- and eighth-grade basketball team consisted of (front row, from left) Garnie "Tootsie" Christian, Freddie Montgomery, Don Mallory, Lyle Sandidge, Paul Chesnutt, Stuart Gray, (second row, from left) Dwain Christian, Harold Patterson, unknown, Wendell Christian and Coach Glen Carroll. Contributed by Barbara Christian Tunnell of Kingsport.

Stepping high

Janice Snyder Barnes was a majorette in the
Dobyns-Bennett High School band in 1957. The
daughter of the late Dewey and Martha Lane
Snyder, she now lives in Georgia. Contributed by
Cathy Johnston, cousin of Janice Snyder Barnes,
of Kingsport.

Dirt track racing

James Eston Trent competed in dirt track racing between 1948 and 1954. He raced in North Carolina, Tennessee, South Carolina, Virginia, Kentucky and Ohio on quarter-mile and half-mile tracks and won several awards. He wore a steel plate on his boot to help as he slid around corners. Contributed by Marie Trent of Kingsport.

Ross Camp Ground team

The 1954 basketball team at Ross Camp Ground Elementary School consisted of (from left) W.N. Ragel, Roy Barbour, David Parton, Don Robinson, Tommy Moffitt, Jim Ashworth, Hubert Barbour, Gerald Parker, Garland Brooks, Bob Sensabaugh, Wayne Carter, Gene Moffitt, Tommy Sensabaugh and M.C. Ray. The Ross Camp Ground School operated from 1940 to 1970. The school building only had four rooms, so the team played outside. Contributed by Don Brooks of Church Hill.

Rising high

The 1953 Church Hill High School football team consisted of (bottom row, from left) Bob Bowen, Zeb Norris (deceased), Norman Tunnell, Bill Horton, (second row, from left) Bill Ball, Bob Chappell, Ken Christian, (third row, from left) John Arnold (deceased), Jim Epperson and (top) Cotton Russell (deceased). Contributed by Norman Tunnell of Kingsport.

Blountville cheerleader

Mary Ann Akard was a cheerleader at Blountville High School throughout her high school career, which included the year 1955. The cheerleading squad cheered just for the basketball team as there was no football team at the time. Contributed by Mary Ann Akard Wininger of Blountville.

Guard at Blountville

Charles Venis Gray played guard for the Blountville High School basketball team all four years he was a student there. He graduated in 1959. Contributed by Cyndee Gray Harr of Blountville.

Award-winning team

The Tennessee Eastman softball team won an award in 1950. Team member Freddie Lee McNutt (standing, fourth from right) was accompanied by his son Larry Gene McNutt. Kelly "Buck" Vermillion Jr. (right) presented the trophy to the team. Contributed by Nancy McNutt Christian of Weber City, Virginia.

Coach Gillespie's team

The circa 1953 or 1954 Lynn Garden Elementary School basketball team consisted of (front row, from left) unknown, Larry Mosley, Jimmy Wells, Ernie Mosley, Jerry Hensley, Coach Cal Gillespie, (seond row, from left) Bobby Herron, Jack Gilliam, Jack Dotson, Jimmy Fletcher, unknown, (third row, from left) Butch White, Johnny Fletcher, Gary Phillips, Dewey Bright and unknown. Contributed by Anita Hall, niece of Jack Gilliam, of Kingsport.

From the bench

The Clintwood High School basketball team bench was eager to get the fourth quarter over in the District 8 game versus Jonesville High School in 1953. Clintwood won the game 53 to 26. Howard Deel (second from right) was the coach at the time and later was principal at Clintwood. He was named to the Virginia Sports Hall of Fame. Sitting to the right of Coach Deel were players Jim Stanley, Darrell Fleming and Carl Hylton. To the left of Coach Dell (at right in photo) was Norman Mullins, his assistant and a teacher at Clintwood. The photo was taken by Frank Creasy. Contributed by Carl Hylton of Kingsport.

From Church Hill to Vanderbilt

Reece Gibson played football at Church Hill High School from 1958 through 1960 and then went on to play at Vanderbilt for two years. He also competed against Joe Namath. Contributed by Keith Gibson of Kingsport.

Go team!

The Lynn View High School cheerleaders in 1955 were (clockwise from bottom) Mary McClellan, Linda Gibson, Betty Bradley, Joan Brooks, Ida Musick, Billie Fagan, Wanda Gilliam and Sue Haulsee. Contributed by Wanda Gilliam Addington of Kingsport.

Kayo team

The Kayo City League basketball team in 1956-57 consisted of (front row, from left) Jack Jones (deceased), Bill Jones and Bob McGlothlin, (back row, from left) Phil McGlothlin (deceased), Jim Davis, Donnie Jones, M.J. Peters (deceased) and Guy "Mule" Crawford (deceased). Kayo was a service station in Weber City, Virginia. All of the team members were from Gate City, Virginia, and East Carters Valley area. Contributed by Jim Davis of Mount Carmel.

On the ball

Wanda Gilliam and Bob Arnold were named Most Athletic of their senior class at Lynn View High School in 1957. Contributed by Wanda Gilliam Addington of Kingsport.

Dobyns Taylor team

The 1954 Dobyns Taylor softball team for the Kingsport City League consisted of (front row, from left) John "Duck" Grills, Shelbourne Wallace, Joe Morley, Roy Huff, (back row, from left) Merle Parker, Ray Collins, Charlie Berry, Powell King, unknown and Bruce Courtney. Contributed by Jack Berry of Jekyll Island, Georgia.

The Blountville Tigers

The 1950 Blountville High School Tigers basketball team consisted of (front row, from left) Coach Bernie Webb, Earl Fleenor, Bruce Wade, Kenneth Wade, Tommy Duff, Bill Cole, Frank Bolling, Fred Barger, (back row, from left) Jack Patrick, Bob Bunn, Clarence Clark, Harry Cross, John Nottingham, Dickie Broyles and Wayne Moody. Contributed by Margie Jennings of Blountville.

Triple threat

Richard "Buddy" Williams, Bill McHorris and Robert "Bobby" Light played baseball for Dobyns-Bennett High School during the 1955-56 season. Contributed by Shirley Light, wife of Bobby Light, of Kingsport.

Talking ball

Dobyns-Bennett High School baseball players Robert "Bobby" Light and John Whited talked a little strategy with legendary Coach Guy G. Crawford for the 1955-56 season. John Whited later coached baseball at the University of Tennessee at Knoxville. Contributed by Shirley Light, wife of Bobby Light, of Kingsport.

U.S. Army team

When Ted Hoover (back row, third from right) served three years in the U.S. Army, he played basketball and softball. While he was serving in Eritrea, East Africa, in 1953, he played on the post's basketball team. The games were played outside on a dirt floor following Olympic rules. Contributed by Ted Hoover of Kingsport.

Keokee basketball

Coach Gilmer Bledose (back row, center) coached the Keokee High School Mountaineers girls' basketball team in Lee County, Virginia, during the 1956-57 season. The team won 15 games and lost five. Contributed by Gilmer Bledsoe of Duffield, Virginia.

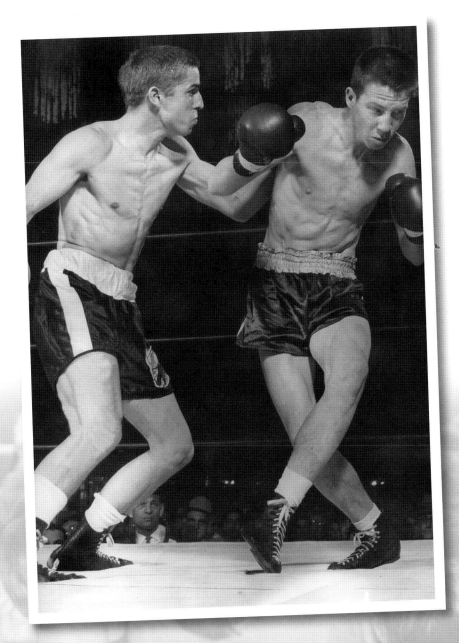

KO'd in second

Buddie Russell, a Golden Gloves boxer from Kingsport, fought Ronald Bowlin in the Golden Gloves Upper Cumberland tournament at the Nashville Hippodrome in 1958. Russell knocked out Bowlin 30 seconds into the second round. Russell won three matches at the Upper Cumberland tournament, allowing him to advance to the Golden Gloves Tournament of Champions in Chicago, where he fought his first and only round the same night as Cassius Clay, who later took the name Muhammad Ali. Contributed by Buddie Russell of Surgoinsville.

African hunt

While serving a three-year stint in the U.S. Army, Ted Hoover spent two and a half years in East Africa, where he had a chance to hunt greater kudu.
Contributed by Ted Hoover of Kingsport.

Lynn View coaches

Carl Matherly (left) and Cecil Puckett were football coaches at Lynn View High School in 1952-53. Contributed by Lou Skeen of Kingsport.

Time for football

Among the members of the Lynn View High School football team in 1952-53 were (from left) Mac Skeen, Howard "Moon Eye" Frazier, Gary Riner, Landin Robinette and Prezzle Quillen. Contributed by Lou Skeen, wife of Mac Skeen, of Kingsport.

First uniforms

Patsy Alley Kilgore was the drum majorette for the Lynn View High School band in 1957. The band was formed in 1956, and got their first uniforms in 1957, which was Patsy's senior year. Contributed by Patsy Kilgore of Kingsport.

Have bat, will play

Jerry Kilgore enjoyed playing baseball in Nickelsville, Virginia, in the early 1950s. Contributed by Jerry Kilgore of Kingsport.

Sevier '57

Cheers for Sevier

The 1957 John Sevier Junior High School cheerleaders were (from left) Sondra Dotson, Pat Muse, Judy Trent, Vivian Eversole, Barbara Williams, Nancy Atkins and Cindy Modlin. The cheerleading coach's daughter, Debbie McJunkin (front), was the squad's mascot. Contributed by Sondra Bridwell of Kingsport.

Panther player

Bill Ball played on the Church Hill High School Panthers football team in the 1950s. The school is now Volunteer High School. Contributed by Shirley Dotson of Kingsport.

Marching on

The Dobyns-Bennett High School majorettes and drum major in 1951 were (from left) Barbara Mercer Cassidy, Johnny Triplette and Joanna Bailey (deceased). They were at Church Circle in downtown Kingsport getting ready to march in the D-B band parade down Broad Street, which was traditionally held before each home football game. Contributed by Shirley Dotson of Kingsport.

RUNNERS UP
HAWKINS COUNTY BASKET BALL TOURNAMENT 1955
ROGERSVILLE TENNESSEE

Tournament play

The 1955 Church Hill Elementary School girls' basketball team, made up of seventh- and eighth-graders, and one sixth-grader, was runner-up in the Hawkins County Basketball Tournament held in Rogersville. The team members were (front row, from left) Mrs. Shanks, Geraldine Huff, Iva Nell Skelton, Joy Bombailey, Ina Woods, Nora Mayo, Brenda Flanigan, Christine Faye Seal, Mr. Figg, (back row, from left) Jean Monroe, Betty Jo Gibbons, Sandra Davis, Sandra Sams and Mrs. Brotherton. Contributed by Sandra Byington of Kingsport.

Play ball on Boggs Hill

Boggs Hill, where the Boggs boys lived, of course, was the site of many a neighborhood ball game in the 1950s, when sandlot baseball was at its best. In 1954, the ball players were (front row, from left) Alvin Wilder, Jim Wells, Gary Peters, the goat mascot, unknown, Dwane Barrett, Lawrence Wilder, Harry Boggs, Charlie Boggs, (back row, from left) Loyd Wilder, Don Bullion, Ron Lingerfelt, Jay Burchett, Tom Boggs, Don Martin, Elwood Peters, Tom Wells, Leonard Kindle and Richard Burchett. Contributed by Jim and Janet Wells of Kingsport.

Let's cheer

Sondra Dotson Bridwell was a cheerleader for John Sevier Junior High in 1957. Contributed by Mary Jane Crawford of Kingsport.

Three coaches

Three of the top coaches in Northeast Tennessee attended the state basketball tournament in Nashville in 1954 and were caught on camera at the Claridge Hotel there. The coaches were Guy Crawford (second from left) of Dobyns-Bennett, Harmon Peters (second from right) of Holston Valley, and John Treadway (background) of Elizabethton. Stan Johnson (left) of D-B, and Billy Smith (right) of Holston Valley were there to play in the tournament. Contributed by Bill Dickson of Kingsport.

State's best

The Dobyns-Bennett High School baseball team won the 1952 state championship beating Memphis Central 3-2. Team captain Buddy Archer accepted the victors' trophy from Webb Porter, assistant secretary for the Tennessee Secondary Schools Athletic Association. The team members were (kneeling, from left) Bill Wilborn; Bodie Scott; Bill Dickson; Oberton "Ougie" Noble; Shelborne Wallace; Frosty Gilliam; Skip Slaughter; H.L. Allen, manager; Lester Gammon, manager; (standing, from left) Buck Collette; Billy Greene; J.R. Maddux; Gardner Hammonds; Coach Guy B. Crawford; Mervin Salley, behind Coach Crawford; Buddy Archer, Donnie Adams; Mr. Porter; Dick Warren; Reece Hefner; Jim Whittle; and Jerry Edwards, manager. Times-News photographer Lyle Byland took the photo. Contributed by Bill Dickson of Kingsport.

Multi-talented athlete

Carroll Dale (No. 10) became most well-known for his football talents, but when he was a student at J.J. Kelly High School in Wise, Virginia, in 1955, he also played basketball, here seen waiting for a rebound in a game against the Appalachia High School Bulldogs. Dale was named to the All-State team in both football and basketball. Contributed by Carroll Dale of Wise, Virginia.

Four Super Bowls

Carroll Dale began his storied football career playing receiver for the J.J. Kelly High School team in Wise, Virginia, in the mid-1950s. Following high school, Dale played for Virginia Tech, and then spent fourteen years in the National Football League, playing first for the Los Angeles Rams from 1960 through 1964, then eight years with the Green Bay Packers, where he was part of three Super Bowl-winning teams in 1965, 1966 and 1967. He finished his career with the Minnesota Vikings, and went out on a high note when the Vikings won the Super Bowl in 1973, his only year with the team. Contributed by Carroll Dale of Wise, Virginia.

Good hands

Carroll Dale played receiver for the J.J. Kelly High School football team in Wise, Virginia, in 1955, and at Virginia Tech. During his fourteen years in the National Football League, Dale played at tight end, flank and wide receiver. He had 438 career receptions and had an average 18.9 yards per reception during his career. He had 52 touchdowns in his career. In addition to being part of four Super Bowl-winning teams, Dale was named to the Pro Bowl in 1968, 1969 and 1970. Contributed by Carroll Dale of Wise, Virginia.

Best athletes

Phyllis Ann Ratliff Marshall and Dean "Jip" Wagner were top athletes at Surgoinsville High School, and were honored with the superlative multiple years -- Marshall in 1952-53, 1953-54 and 1954-55, and Wagner in 1953-54 and 1954-55. Both graduated in 1955. Marshall was a top athlete even in her elementary school days and was named All-Tournament from the A Team in 1948-49 at Liberty Hill Elementary School, Mount Carmel. At Surgoinsville High, she broke the school record by pouring in 41 points to lead her team against Mosheim 50-49 on its home floor in 1955. Wagner, an excellent all-around player, was killed in a car accident while serving in the U.S. Navy soon after he graduated from high school. Contributed by Phyllis Ann Ratliff Marshall of Surgoinsville.

VINCENT STATEN   PITCHER
N. Y. YANKEES   PITCHER

His own card

Not content with just collecting other players' baseball cards, Vince Staten decided in 1958 to create his own baseball card, using a Yankees pitcher card. He wanted a batting pose, but since the photo was taken inside his mother's kitchen, and he was not allowed to swing a bat in the house, Staten had to settle for a pitcher's pose. Staten and his friends enjoyed playing sandlot baseball throughout their boyhood. Contributed by Vince Staten of Kingsport.

Navy football

While serving in the U.S. Navy and stationed at the Little Creek base in Virginia in 1957, Ralph Goins (No. 15), seen here with his coaches, played football for the Little Creek Gators. Contributed by Jenny Harr of Church Hill.

Uniform day

John Sharrett was a rising sophomore and trumpet player in the Ketron High School Band in July 1959. The band had received its first uniforms in time for Kingsport's Fourth of July parade, but, unfortunately, the uniforms were for winter not summer. Nonetheless, the band wore their new uniforms in the parade, which as it does today, started in front of the then-John Sevier Junior High School, now the Kingsport Renaissance Center. Contributed by John Sharrett of Kingsport.

Headed for a touchdown

Ralph Goins dove for a touchdown during a 1953 game at Omer High School in West Virginia. Goins later coached football at the Boys Club, leading teams to several undefeated seasons. He also was an umpire for regional middle school games. Contributed by Jenny Harr of Church Hill.

Seeing the Owls

The members of the 1958 Owls football team at Brookside Elementary School, located off Bloomingdale Road in Sullivan County, were (front row, from left) Charles Thomas, tight end; Kenneth Sexton, right tackle; Dickie Jones, right guard; John Allen Compton, center; Tommy Luster, left guard; Boots Thomas, left tackle; Bobby Nottingham, tight end; (second row) Larry Lavendier, quarterback; (back row, from left) Albert Williams, right halfback; and Tommy Walters, left halfback. The name of the fullback is unknown. Dickie Jones played football at Ketron High School and East Tennessee State University, and coached at Sullivan North, Sullivan South, Sullivan Central, Cherokee, old Rogersville, Twin Springs, Lynn View and Morristown East high schools. John Allen Compton coached football at Sullivan South and retired as athletic director from South in 2008. Contributed by Tana Jones, wife of Dickie Jones, of Rogersville.

On track

Gene Hilton ran track for Dobyns-Bennett High School in 1953, 1954 and 1955. He also played football at Dobyns-Bennett. He was a running back and was varsity captain of the team. Contributed by Jolene Hilton of Kingsport.

Starting lineup

The starting lineup of the boys basketball team at Liberty Hill Elementary School, Mount Carmel, in 1955 consisted of Johnny McClellan, Otis Johnson (deceased), Baxter Trent (deceased), Roy Russell (deceased) and Jimmy Ball. Most of these eighth-graders also went on to play basketball at Church Hill High School. Contributed by Doris Thompson Reaves of Gray.

Three-year letterman

Larry Hixson played guard for the Sullivan High School Pirates from 1952-55. He lettered all three years. Contributed by Henrietta Hixson of Kingsport.

Sullivan football

Donnie Bishop was a block back for the Sullivan High School football team in 1954. He later played football and was a pitcher for a baseball team during his service in the U.S. Air Force. He retired from Tennessee Eastman and still lives in Kingsport. Contributed by Abeleen Bishop of Kingsport.

Relaxing day of golf

Fred Saylor (right), Bud Milhorn, unknown, Blev Rogers, Brad Davidson and (first name unknown) Rogers, all employees of the former Blue Ridge Glass Co., enjoyed a day of golf in the early 1950s on Webster's Golf Course at the Kingsport Country Club, located on what is now the Green Acres and Greenfield neighborhoods in Kingsport. Contributed by Kathy Hawk of Kingsport.

Amazing arm

Ned Jilton, seen here in 1952 at J. Fred Johnson Stadium in Kingsport, was an accomplished pitcher and hitter from his earliest days with Science Hill High School on through his play in the minor leagues from 1943 to 1953. At 16, he was signed by the Columbus, Ohio, Cardinals but was optioned to the Johnson City Cardinals of the Appalachian League, where by July 19, 1943, he was second in the league in strike-outs. Later in 1943 he was called up to Lynchburg, Virginia, in the Piedmont League. When he returned to Johnson City in 1944, he was soon at the top of the league in strike-outs. When he went to Allenton, Pennsylvania, of the Inter-State League later that year, in a game against league-leading Hagerstown, Jilton was the winning pitcher, striking out four, walking one and giving up six hits while going the distance, but he was three for four at the plate with two singles and a double while driving in three runs. After thirteen games at Allentown, he had a .474 batting average. Jilton played at Nashville; Hagerstown, Maryland; Davenport; Macon, Georgia; Portsmouth, Virginia; and Saltville, Virginia, before coming to the Kingsport Cherokees, the Appalachian League's worst team, in 1950. But in 1951, Leo "Muscle" Shoals, one of the best home-run hitters in the history of the minor leagues, came to Kingsport, and between Jilton's pitching and Shoals' hitting, they turned Kingsport from worst to first in the league. Jilton went to Rock Hill, South Carolina, in 1952, but returned to finish his minor-league career in Kingsport in 1953. Contributed by Ned Jilton II of Johnson City.

Liberty Hill basketball

The 1955 Liberty Hill Elementary School girls basketball team included (front row, from left) Joyce Lawson, Josephine Rogers, Scheryl McMillan, Brenda Lockhart, Jo Ann Stallard, Shelby Stacy, and (back row, left) Joyce Morelock. Contributed by Johnny McClellan of Mount Carmel.

The kickoff

Larry Nottingham (left) and Chuck McClellan, 13, enjoyed playing football near their homes in 1957. Contributed by Chuck McClellan of Mount Carmel.

Successful tenure

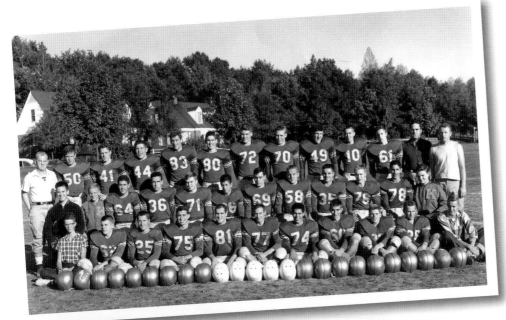

The 1954 Dobyns-Bennett High School football team was the first team coached by then-new coaches Alex Williams and James Hoggatt. During their four-year tenure, D-B won four conference championships while posting thirty-five wins, three losses and two ties. The 1955 team was undefeated and finished second in the state. The 1956 team posted another undefeated season marred only by a 6-6 tie against rival Chattanooga Central. The 1957 team came up on the short end of a 28-27 contest against Chattanooga Central. Jerry Gilmer (No. 76) played for Williams and Hoggatt for three years. Contributed by Jerry Gilmer of Watauga, Tenn.

Cheering them on

The Lynn View High School cheerleaders in 1951-52 were (front row, from left) Patsy Bellamy, Bill Allen, Shirley Quillen, (back row, from left) Sue Lackey, Katherine Copas, Jean Coates, Peggy Smith and Zella Heaberlin (not pictured). Contributed by Jean (Coates) Blessing of Kingsport.

Marching leaders

Alfred Newton was the Shoemaker High School band's drum major and Charlotte Quillen (left) was one of three majorettes from 1949 through 1953. The other two majorettes' names are unknown. Contributed by Herbert J. McClelland of Kingsport.

Long-time director

Katherine Greene Beal (standing right) founded the Kingsport Junior High School band in 1946 and was director of both the John Sevier and Ross N. Robinson junior high schools bands. This photo shows Mrs. Beal with the 1958-59 Sevier band. Contributed by Richard Brown, Sevier Middle School band director, of Kingsport.

Halftime peace time

During halftime of a charity basketball game that pitted alumni of Shoemaker High School against the Oklahoma Indians, the two teams sat down and shared a "peace pipe." Taking part in the ceremony was Shoemaker alumnus Bill Baldwin (center). Contributed by Herbert J. McClelland of Kingsport.

Perfect record

The Rogersville High School basketball B team was undefeated in 1954, beating Knoxville South, Dobyns-Bennett, Rush Strong, Bristol, Cosby, Johnson City, Greeneville, Morristown, Sullivan High, Baileyton, Boones Creek, Bluff City, Lynn View, Newport, Mosheim and Church Hill. The team members were (from left) Daryl Alvis, Jim Rogan, Donald Robertson, Buddy Price, Ronald Brooks, Allen Brewer, George Davis, Billy McMakin and Wayne Haun. Contributed by Wayne Haun of Surgoinsville.

Mayes, Wayne Haun, Whitty Lane, Andy Childerss, Bud Price, Mole Winstead, Ron Brooks, Chief Robertson, Pete Rogan, Daryl Al.

State tournament team

The 1956-57 Rogersville High School basketball team went to the state tournament. The team won the district tournament, defeating Bulls Gap, Baileyton, Surgoinsville and Greeneville. It was runner-up in the regional tournament, defeating Sevierville and Elizabethton, and losing in the final to Blountville. In the state tournament at the Vanderbilt gymnasium in Nashville, the Warriors won over Paris Grove but lost in overtime to Linden, the state champions. The team members were Lewis Mayes, Wayne Haun, Whitty Lane, Andy Childress, Bud Price, Gerald Winstead, Ron Brooks, Chief Robertson, Pete Rogan and Daryl Alvis. Co-captains Ronald Brooks and Gerald Winstead were named to the Conference, All-District, All-Regional and All-State teams. Contributed by Lewis Mayes of Rogersville.

Cheering for the winners

The Holston High School 1953 cheerleaders were (from left) Louise Fink Shaffer, Betty Jane Gentry Jones (deceased), Dorothy Marsh Loy, Catherine Slaughter Gilbert and Mary Helen Baldwin Swanay. The cheerleaders most enjoyed cheering their team on to victory. Holston High School was located in Blountville and later was combined with Blountville High School into Sullivan Central High School. Contributed by Mary Helen B. Swanay of Kingsport.

Holston High basketball

The members of the 1953 Holston High School basketball team were (front row, from left) Donnie Doran, Tommy Cross, Robert Wagner, Denver King (deceased), Bill Hamilton, Coach S.C. "Dottie" Rutherford (deceased), (second row, from left) Kenneth Eldridge (deceased), Phil Bowery, Pete Coates, Ronnie Salts (deceased), Tommy Wright and Wayne Jones, manager. Contributed by Mary Helen B. Swanay of Kingsport.

Blowing their horns

The horn section of the 90-piece Lynn View High School Band was handsomely dressed for its 1957 yearbook photo in uniforms paid for from funds raised by the Band Boosters Club, which organized the band in 1954. The horn section consisted of (front row, from left) Tommy Boggs, Judy Anderson, Janice Powers, Jimmy Catron, Shelby Vicars, Nellie Smith, Brenda Peters, Ernestine Lovin, (second row, from left) Nancy Fugate, Don Lovin, Lamar Hamilton, Sarah Lee Shearer, Linda Carter (deceased), Verlene Bond, Peggy Crawford, Janice Culbertson, (back row, from left) Jimmy McConnell, Tommy Hamilton and Freddie Addington. Mr. Witt was the band director. Contributed by Janice Culbertson Jones, Gate City, Va., whose mother Ruby Blankenship Culbertson gave much of her time to working on fund-raising events for the Band Boosters Club.

Hilton girls basketball

The members of the 1953-54 Hilton High School basketball team members were (front row, from left) Barbara Pannell Kilbourne, Mary Lynn Worley Booher, Freda Hunsucker Barb, Joyce Gray Manis, Gracie Smith Dowell, Marie Carter Washburn, (back row, from left) Coach Dwight Mason, Phyllis Thomas Snodgrass, Roberta Blackburn Stewart, Nancy Dougherty Godsey, Catherine Godsey Crooke, Peggy Gardner Bays, Jane Gardner Sapp and Shirley Weatherly Salyer, manager. Contributed by Joyce Gray Manis of Kingsport.

Hilton High's best

Joe Blackburn and Joyce Gray were voted Most Athletic by their classmates in 1954 at Hilton High School in Virginia. Contributed by Joyce Gray Manis of Kingsport.

Herschel Cooper (kneeling, third from left) was a member of the Kingsport Press softball team in the late 1950s and early 1960s. Contributed by Jacquie Dishner, sister of Herschel Cooper, of Blountville.

Dungannon baseball

The 1957 Dungannon, Virginia, baseball team, consisted of (front row, from left) Lee Stallard, Richard Horton, Allan Hillman, Noah Sluss, (second row, from left) Virgil Gillenwater, Coach Jack Dixon and Tommy Gillenwater. Contributed by Phyllis McNew Nitschke of Kingsport.

Eagles fly again

The 1959 Dungannon Eagles basketball team consisted of (standing, from left) Johnny Flanary, Mike Blackwell, Richard Horton, James Jennings, Jimmy Flanary, Kenneth Wolfe, Jim Scott, Bobby Whetsel and Roger Wolfe. Mr. Gwinn was the coach. Contributed by Phyllis McNew Nitschke of Kingsport.

Godsey brothers

The Godsey brothers made up nearly a third of the Jaycees Little League team in Gate City, Virginia, in 1969. Jerry Godsey (standing, third from left) and Hugh Godsey (standing, fifth from left) made the All-Star team in 1969. Harold Godsey (sitting, left) and Larry Godsey (sitting, fifth from left) made the All-Star team in 1970. Their father Allen Godsey (standing, left) was the coach. Contributed by Nancy Godsey, mother of the boys and wife of the coach, of Gate City.

Swim lesson

Coach Frank Nauss taught six boys, including Raymond Gregory (second from right) and Shelby "Buddy" Gregory (third from right) how to do the freestyle stroke in 1969 at the Dobyns-Bennett High School pool. Contributed by Diane Purdy of Kingsport.

Won two conferences

Vernon Patrick played tackle for the Ketron High School football team from 1963 through 1965. All three years, the team won both the Upper Lakes and Rotherwood conferences. Contributed by Karen Patrick of Hiltons, Virginia.

Award-winning linebacker

Dickie Jones, who stood five feet and eleven and a half inches, played linebacker and center for the Ketron High School football team in the early 1960s. He was a letterman each year from 1960 to 1963; was a member of the 100 Tackle Club, having made 120 tackles; and was named to the Knoxville News-Sentinel's All East Tennessee team, the 1963 Best Offensive Lineman, the 1963 Most Valuable Lineman, to the 1963 Coaches All Rotherwood Conference team; and to the Times-News All Rotherwood Conference team. Contributed by Casey Jones of Rogersville.

Gravely basketball

The 1961-62 Gravely Elementary School basketball team consisted of (back row, from left) David Vicars, Vernon Patrick, Denny Joe Garber, Coach John D. Miller, Jimmy McGhee, Terry Lawson, Bernard Johnson, (front row, from left) (first name unknown) Fortner, (first name unknown) Vicars, (first name unknown) McLain, (first name unknown) Russell, Larry Knowles, unknown and Wayne Light. John D. Miller also was the school's principal. Contributed by Karen Patrick of Hiltons, Virginia.

Cornet player

Carole Ann Wright played cornet in the John Sevier Junior High School Band for three years. This photo from 1961 shows her in her band uniform. Contributed by Carole Ann Wright Tipton of Kingsport.

In the big leagues

When Kingsport native Charlie Leonard (right) was called up to play in the Pittsburgh Pirates minor league organization in 1961, one of his teammates was Bob Bailey, a native of California, who received a $175,000 bonus upon signing, which at that time was the largest bonus in history. In fact Bailey's father quit his job in California just to manage his son's money. Leonard and Bailey played Triple-A baseball together for two years in Asheville and in Columbus, Ohio. Bailey went on to play for sixteen years in the major leagues. Contributed by Charlie Leonard of Jonesborough.

Soap Box derby champ

In 1967, Anthony Shipley won the Tri-Cities Soap Box Derby in Bristol in a car sponsored by the Optimist Club. He went on to compete at the national derby, which was held in Akron, Ohio. Contributed by Susan Shipley of Kingsport.

McPheeters Bend softball

The 1962 McPheeters Bend softball team in the Hawkins County Recreation League won a lot of games with players (front row, from left) Dorthy Patterson, Brenda Marshall, Kay Dobbs, Betty Jo Smith, Evelyn Arnold, (back row, from left) Coach Jimmy Patterson, unknown, Ann Derrick, Edith Wallen, Beulah Arnold, Pat Parson, Blanch Craddock and Coach Clyde Craddock. Contributed by Beulah Arnold of Church Hill, who played second base.

Y'all come bowling

The Women's International Bowling Congress was held in Memphis in 1963 and competing on the national tournament team from Kingsport's Warpath Lanes were (from left) Thelma Jones, Frances Lane, Edna Simpson, Wanda Kilbourn and Frances Stapleton. Contributed by Frances Lane of Kingsport.

Junior bowling winners

In 1962, Linda Stapleton (left) and Dennis Lane were the American Junior Bowling Congress national mixed doubles champions. They were coached by Dennis Lane's mother, Frances Lane. Contributed by Frances Lane of Kingsport.

True dedication

Even though David Cole had already graduated from Lynn View High School in spring 1965, his band director Ray Witt called him at the end of June and asked him to return to play bass drum in the Kingsport Fourth of July parade as no one else was available to play the instrument. Contributed by David Cole of Kingsport.

Love of bowling

Thomas Moffitt enjoyed bowling as a hobby in the late 1960s in Kingsport. He participated in several leagues. Contributed by Mary (Spears) Bloomer, aunt of Thomas Moffitt, of Church Hill.

First band of Cougars

Pattie Glover was among the first members of the Sullivan Central High School band, when the school opened in the 1968-69 school year. After playing trombone at Blountville High School for three years, she played chimes for the Central band. She was part of the first graduating class at Central. Contributed by Pattie Glover Dillman of Piney Flats.

Words of wisdom

Gate City High School quarterback Mike Foster got some sound advice from long-time Coach Harry Fry during a 1967 football game. Foster later played quarterback at Emory & Henry College. Contributed by Jody Hamilton of Kingsport.

Avid hunter

In 1960, Beulah Arnold was an avid hunter at turkey shoots. Contributed by Beulah Arnold of Church Hill.

On defense

The Lynn View High School football team's defensive line in 1967 consisted of (from left) Billy Greer, Tommy Horton, Sam Patterson (deceased), Eugene Bellamy, Eddie Thomas, Steve Ray, Tim Gilliam, Phil Pendergrass and Jimmy McConnell. Contributed by Steve Ray of Blountville.

From D-B to E&H

After playing on the Dobyns-Bennett High School state championship football teams in 1959 and 1960, Jerry Beck played for Emory & Henry College. Beck is now a Circuit Court Judge for Sullivan County. Contributed by Jerry Beck of Kingsport.

Parade ready

Suzanne Parris Lyon (left) played clarinet in the Lynn View High School Band, and her sister Donna Parris Mullins was a twirler with Mary Hamilton's Twirlettes. Both marched in the Christmas parade in 1962. Contributed by Helen Parris of Kingsport.

League winners

In June 1961, the bowling team of (front row, from left) Bill Sampson (deceased), Bill Bellamy (deceased), (back row, from left) Worley Lane, Archie Smith (deceased) and Harold Gibson (deceased) won their winter league. The team was sponsored by S&S Garage. Contributed by Connie A. Walton of Kingsport.

Multi-talented athlete

David Gladson was a multi-talented athlete at Rogersville High School, playing quarterback for the football team, as well as playing for the basketball, baseball, golf and track teams. Sadly, his athletic career was cut short when he was killed in a car accident at age 15 in 1969, when this photo was taken. Contributed by Brenda Gladson of Rogersville.

All-Star

David Gladson made the Babe Ruth All-Star team in July 1969. In addition to playing baseball, he also played football, basketball and golf, and ran track. He died in a car accident later that year. He was 15. Contributed by Larry Gladson of Rogersville.

Midget league baseball

The 1962 Eagles Midget League baseball team, which competed in the Kingsport City League, consisted of (front row, from left) Joel Wooten, Dale Richardson, Dickie Kilgore, Mike Leach, Tommy Blankenbeckler, Mike Kilgore, (back row, from left) Joe Meach, Phil Pendergrass, Rusty Canter, Coach Gene Hammonds, John Palmer, Mike Sykes, Larry Donihe, Coach Graham Pendergrass and David Cloninger. Contributed by David Cloninger of Kingsport.

Connie Mack league

Kingsport's Connie Mack League team was the Upper East Tennessee champion and second in the state in 1969, winning seventeen games and losing five. The team members were (front row, from left) Hershel Helton, Don Starrette, Billy Bray, Bill Neurdenburg, Gary Chesney, Gary Hale, Mike Babb, Randy Shipley, (second row, from left) Head Coach Clyde Starrette, Sammy Norris, Tony Blakley, Mike Hensley, George Penn, David Hoover, Steve Bailey, Steve Thornburg, Tim Hale, and Assistant Coach Harold Mills. Other team members who are not pictured were Powell Moore, Dean Jones, David Overby and Assistant Coach Jim Herbert. Contributed by Gary Chesney of Morristown.

Playing for Hokies

After graduating from Dobyns-Bennett High School in 1964, Jud Brownell played defensive end at Virginia Teach from 1965 through 1969, and was a starter three of those four years. He played in two Liberty Bowls with Frank Beamer, now head coach at Virginia Tech, and defended Ole Miss quarterback Archie Manning. Against the legendary Bear Bryant's Alabama team, he scored the only touchdown for the Hokies after recovering a blocked punt in the end zone. That made him the leading scorer for the game, and he was on defense. He graduated from Virginia Tech in 1970 with a bachelor's degree in mechanical enginnering and now works as a real estate appraiser in Kingsport. Contributed by Cathy Brownell of Kingsport.

Church league champions

The Blountville Christian Church basketball team won the Blountville Church League in 1967. The team members were (front row, from left) Scott Webb, Tony Morton, Tony Jones, (second row, from left) Coach Allen Glover, Joey Holt, Ronnie Milhorn, Jeff Barger, David Webb, (back row, from left) Mike Glover, Ricky Bunn, Tony Barger, Junior Payne and Dickie Bunn. Six of the team members still belong to Blountville Christian Church. Contributed by Mike Glover, son of Allen Glover, of Blountville.

Tiny twirlers

Donna Brooks Shipley and Tina Brooks Henderson did twirling for three years with the Church Hill Twirlettes. Their instructor was Brenda Russell and they often demonstrated their skills in the Fourth of July and Christmas parades. Contributed by Tina Henderson of Surgoinsville.

Homemade jerseys

The Celtics, who played in the Kingsport Recreation Department's Pee Wee basketball league in the early 1960s, had jerseys that featured "C's" that were cut from felt and stitched onto the team members' shirts by their mothers. The team members were (from left) David Phillips, Tigger Poole, Paul Williams, Wally Boyd, Danny Dietrich, Steve Scott, Doug Sullins, Don Spann and Bobby Snapp. They were coached by David Ross (back). Contributed by Tina Henderson of Surgoinsville.

Tennis awards

At the Optimist Tennis Tournament awards ceremony in 1964, Miss Kingsport, Vicki Hurd Bartholomew, who later was first runner-up in the 1964 Miss America Pageant, was on hand to present awards to the players, who included Robert A. Brown (second row, third from left), Dickie George (second row, fourth from left), Martha Slemp (first row, second from right), Linda Shoun (first row, third from right) and Trey Tylie (first row, second from left). William K. Brown (front row, right) and Al Wilkes Sr. (front row, left) were instrumental in starting tennis in Kingsport in the 1950s. Linda Shoun and Dickie George would later marry. Contributed by Becky Brown of Kingsport.

Bowling down South

Mildred Smith (second, from left), Dot Horton and Bill Whetsel were among a team from Kingsport that bowled at the Women's International Bowling Congress on May 10, 1966 in New Orleans. The two women on either end are unidentified. The team bowled regularly at Warpath Lanes in Kingsport. Contributed by Dot Horton of Kingsport.

Jaycees Little League

Among the members of the 1966 Gate City Jaycees Little League team were Lindy Collins (front row, third from left), DeWayne Hall (front row, right) and Carl Perry (second row, left). The team was coached by Jerry Hall (back row, left). Contributed by Frankie Collins of Weber City, Virginia.

Power cheering

Ready for their next game, the Church Hill Elementary School cheerleaders in 1962 were (front row, from left) Judy Christian Stewart, unknown, Linda Watterson, Patricia Messick Turner, (back row, from left) Jane Cooper Crawford, Patsy Fields Jones, Joyce Porter Overbey, Ruth Simpson Lemmons, Judy Bishop Christian and Susan Taylor Redwine. Contributed by Jane Crawford of Kingsport.

Ready to shoot

Larry Crawford played guard for the John Sevier Junior High School basketball team in 1961. He was coached by Tommy Wray. Contributed by Jane Crawford of Kingsport.

Called up

Jimmy Cooper (center) was just an eighth-grader in 1967 when he was asked to play on the Church Hill High School golf team, which was coached by Clyde Brooks (left) and Jerry Hutson (right). The other team members were (from left) Walter Bagley, Joel Bailey, James Moles and Comet Harper. Contributed by Jim Cooper of Kingsport.

Three-year starter

Tommy Bryant played four years and started three for the Rye Cove High School football team, which he played for in the late 1960s. He played halfback and middle linebacker. Contributed by Tommy Bryant of Church Hill.

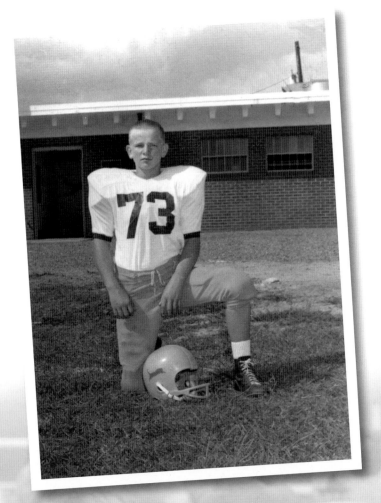

Sox baseball

Jerry Lynn Ketron played for the Sox in Little League baseball when he was a seventh-grader at Kingsley Elementary School in August 1966. He played third base in Little League and at Ketron High School. He now lives in Mount Carmel. Contributed by Janie Ketron, mother of Jerry Lynn Ketron, of Kingsport.

Growth spurt

When Jim Hall joined the Church Hill High School Panther football team in 1969, he weighed in at 99 pounds. During his senior year, he topped 200 pounds. Contributed by Grace Hall Hayes of Kingsport.

Merchants' league

Lowell Fletcher (left), Gilmer Lane, Lee Prillhart, Ira Ramsey and Sneed Stuffle bowled together in the Bowl-Mor Merchants' League in the early to mid-1960s. The five men began bowling after forming a friendship through church. Contributed by Barbara Lane, wife of Gilmer Lane, of Kingsport.

Magnavox team

Ralph Goins (front row, left) played baseball with the Greeneville Magnavox team in 1962. Contributed by David Goins of Church Hill.

New meet record

In February 1964, S.D. Dean, who ran the mile and half-mile for Dobyns-Bennett High School's track team, set the new meet record in the mile, 4:41.7, at the Chattanooga Indoor High School track meet. That 30-year-old record was the oldest record standing when Dean broke it. In addition to running track, Dean also ran cross country for D-B. He was offered six track scholarships, and ran on scholarship at East Tennessee State University from 1965 to 1967. Contributed by S.D. Dean of Kingsport.

Co-MVP

When Church Hill High School met Science Hill High School in the 1962 Exchange Bowl, Conley E. Bailey, who played fullback for Church Hill, shared the trophy for most valuable player with Steve Spurrier of Science Hill (not pictured). Bailey played all four years at Church Hill. Contributed by Barbara Bellamy of Gate City, Virginia.

The Ripper

Jack "The Ripper" Milhorn was a top basketball player for Holston High School in Blountville in the mid- to late 1960s. Though standing just five feet, eleven inches, he had a 40-inch vertical leap. He was the winner of the 1967-68 Upper Lakes Conference scoring title with a 24.9 point average. During a game against Washington College Academy, he scored 40 points, and in another game he came within five points of the school's scoring record for rebounds with 23. In addition to basketball, he played baseball, and was on the track and field team for Holston High, from which he graduated in 1968. He was recruited by Villanova University, but chose to play basketball at Milligan College. Contributed by Jacki Bragg, daughter of Jack Milhorn, of Blountville.

Wallace News team

The Kingsport City League basketball team sponsored by Wallace News in 1961-62 consisted of (front row, from left) Radall Shelton, Preston Brockman, Eddie Arnold, Ron Ramey, (back row, from left) Coach Cel Crum, Jerry Laningham, James Gillenwater, Johnny Stevens and John Dunnivant. Cel Crum owned Wallace News and also was the public address announcer at Dobyns-Bennett High School ball games. Contributed by Jerry Laningham of Church Hill.

Coach-players reunion

Coach Tom Brixey (center), an alumnus of the University of Tennessee and the then football coach at Dobyns-Bennett High School in 1966, visited two of his former D-B players, Nick Showalter (left) and Victor "Vick" Dingus while they were playing at UT. Contributed by Mark Dingus of Blountville.

Flag swingers

The Dobyns-Bennett High Schoool marching band flag swingers in 1960 were (from left) Jinx Christensen, Katherine Looney, Mary Parsons and Judy Noel Bowery. Contributed by Willard Bowery of Kingsport.

In memoriam

Johnson Memorial Stadium in Church Hill, was named in memory of Mike Johnson who played at Church Hill High School and played linebacker and center at the University of South Carolina with Dan Reeves at quarterback. Johnson was expected to receive All-American honors but battled cancer during his junior year and died in September 1965. Contributed by Jack Jarvis, cousin of Mike Johnson, of Kingsport.

First Surgoinsville team

Football came to Surgoinsville High School for the first time in 1969. The team consisted of (front row, from left) David Quarry, Mickey Jones, Roger Davis, Kris Carr, Mike Allen, Jerry Henderson, Daniel Snapp, Gary Henderson, David Elkins, H.J. Allen, David Armstrong, Mike Winegar, H.L. Bailey, (second row, from left) Jonathan Case, James Gillis, Gary Mullins, John M. Patterson, Randall Brown, Keith Sorah, Johnny Huff, Jack Case, Randy Henry, Leon Hickman, Clay Carr, Gary Case, Eugene Housewright, (third row, from left) Assistant Coach Delmar Gillenwater, Assistant Coach Lynn Skelton, Greg Golden, Eddie Bowery, Ronnie Greer, Steve Horne, Dennis Anderson, Tommy Eidson, Allen Siverts, Keith Lipe, Mitch McGee, Alan Armstrong and Head Coach Jim Anderson. Contributed by Debbie Greer of Surgoinsville.

Unbeaten but second

Dobyns-Bennett High School's football first team went 10-0-1 in 1965-66, which actually was a disappointing year because the 1964 team had won the state championship. The one tying game put D-B in second place for the season. The team consisted of (front row, from left) Vic Dingus, David Postell, Tony Grills, Boyd Page, Jim Minnick, Don Burke, Doug Dellinger, (second row) Tommy England, (third row, from left) David Piercy, Larry McClellan and Ken Brockman. Contributed by Doug Dellinger of Kingsport.

Eagles basketball

The Surgoinsville High School Eagles basketball team in 1961-62 consisted of (front row, from left) Fayne Cooper, Colby Reeves, Dennis Bellamy, J.E. Mauk, Steve Lytton, (second row, from left) Coach Jim Fleming, Jimmy Lynn Greer, Gene Skelton, Don Lawson, Dwight Carpenter, Stanley Taylor and Coach Daugherty. Contributed by June Taylor of Surgoinsville.

Still cheering

The 1960-63 Surgoinsville High School cheerleaders are still cheering together and are still fast friends. The team consisted of (from left) Kathy Rose Bailey Finke, Betty Sue Allen Johnson, Linda K. Greer Kimbro, Sandra Faye Charles Culbertson, Norma Jean Burchfield Johnson and Nancy Mullins Gray. Contributed by Linda Kimbro of Surgoinsville.

Playing cousins

Michael Manis and his cousin Randy Manis enjoyed playing a little backyard baseball in 1967 in Falls Church, Virginia, where they both lived at the time. Michael now lives in Kingsport, and Randy lives in the Nashville area. Contributed by Michael Manis of Kingsport.

Close-knit squad

The Ketron High School Wildcats cheerleaders in 1968-69 were a close-knit squad that loved cheering both football and basketball games. The squad members were (front row, from left) Pat Leftwich, Rachel Breeding, Gale Tate, Brenda Tate, (second row, from left) Sherry Bell, Sharon Stuffle, Patty Richards and Linda Depew. Contributed by Pat (Richards) Dellinger of Kingsport.

Legendary coach

Harry Fry (center) was a legendary coach at Gate City High School. Among the players he coached were Jeff Baker (left) and Tommy Godsey. Contributed by Brent Roberts of Gate City, Virginia.

Warming up

Johnny Sanders Jr. (right) ran to warm up for a Gate City High School Blue Devils football game during the 1974-75 season. Gate City won the state championship that year. Contributed by Diana Meredith of Kingsport.

For posterity

Jim Roberts (front row, left), Coach Harry Fry, Stanley Jenkins, Von McConnell (back row, left) and Johnny Sanders Jr., were getting ready for the football season in August 1976 when this photo for the Gate City High School Blue Devils yearbook was taken. Contributed by Diana Meredith of Kingsport.

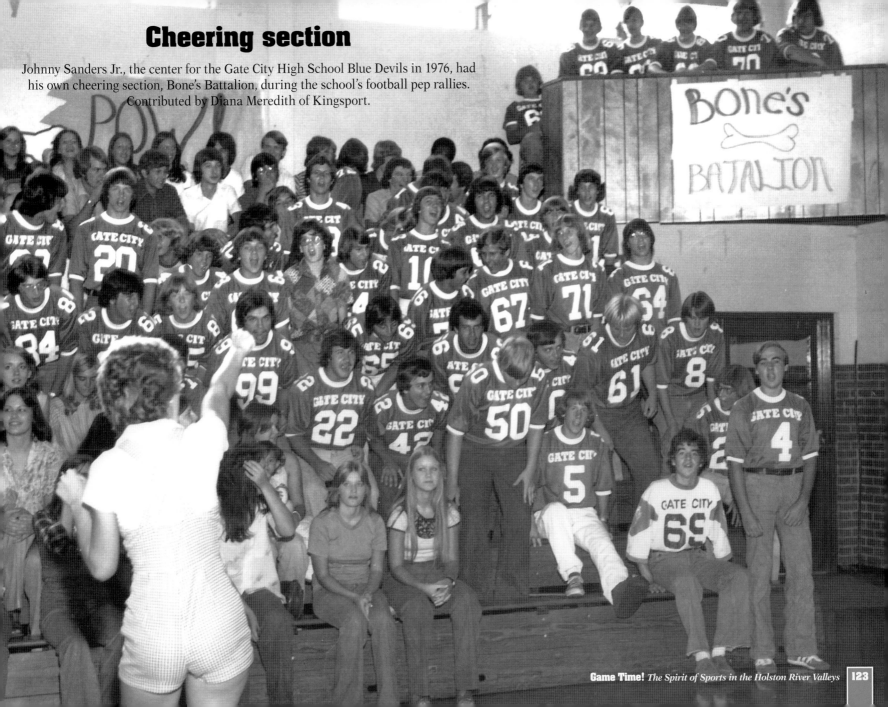

Cheering section

Johnny Sanders Jr., the center for the Gate City High School Blue Devils in 1976, had his own cheering section, Bone's Battalion, during the school's football pep rallies. Contributed by Diana Meredith of Kingsport.

Team captain

In 1976, Johnny Sanders Jr., was captain of the Gate City High School Blue Devils football team. Sanders began playing organized football with the Gate City Little League's East End Redskins. He moved up through the Gate City football program until he reached the high school level where he was coached by Hall of Fame Coach Harry Fry and mentor defensive coach Joe Rusek, to whom he gives much credit for his success on the field. Sanders played center and defensive end and was part of the 1974 state championship team. He was named All Southwest Virginia Defensive End in 1976. Contributed by Lisa Sanders of Gate City, Virginia.

State semis

On November 23, 1974, Gate City High School played Amherst High School in the state semi-finals at Gate City, pitting the Blue Bandit Defense against the Amherst Lancers. Gate City won 71-17. Among the Gate City players who contributed to that victory were (from left) Rick Shoemaker (No. 60), Terry Frazier (No. 72), Tim Blankenbeckler (No. 31), David Wolfe (No. 83), Rick Begley (No. 66), and Brian Seaver (No. 11). Contributed by Terry Frazier of Gate City, Virginia.

The Other Mother

Frances Ann Culbertson, a teacher at Gate City High School, was the football team's "other mother," during her tenure at the school. In 1976, she mothered (front row, from left) Mike Clark, Randy Clark, Von McConnell, Aaron Smith, (back row, from left) Jim Roberts, Johnny Sanders Jr., Nick Moore, Stanley Jenkins and Gary Darter. Contributed by Lisa Sanders of Gate City, Virginia.

Basketball trio

Hugh Godsey (left), Ryland Craft and David Wolfe played basketball for Gate City High School in 1975 under Coach John Vicars (not pictured). Contributed by Nancy Godsey of Gate City, Virginia.

Sevier vs. Robinson

Long-time rivals John Sevier and Ross N. Robinson middle schools met on the baseball field in 1977 at John Sevier Middle School. John Blessing (left) was Sevier's catcher and John Gray was at bat for Robinson. Sevier's coach, John Rippatoe, is seated on the bench at far right. RNR's head coach, Larry Overbey, is in the background behind the batter. Contributed by John Blessing of Kingsport.

World record

In 1972, Shelby Gregory (standing, second from left), Dana Goodwin, Rick Hutson and Miles Burdine decided to break the world record for continuous swimming of four days. They swam for 168 hours (or 273 miles) with two boys swimming in four-hour blocks of 30 minutes on and 30 minutes off, breaking the world record. WKPT broadcast poolside for much of the event, and when the foursome did break the record, all three major networks were at the pool to cover the story. To honor their world record, then-Tennessee Gov. Winfield Dunn (left) presented the four with a certificate. Contributed by Diane Purdy of Kingsport.

Long Island volleyball

The Long Island Elementary School Tigers volleyball team were the 1979 and 1980 Sullivan County volleyball champions. The members of the 1979 team were (front row, from left) Tammy Hale, Tracy Hutson, Anna Dykes, Flora Johnson, Sherry Johnson, (back row, from left) Kim Manis, Mickey Ketron, Donna Stapleton, Ginger Condry and Coach David Wade. Contributed by Judy Hale, mother of Tammy Hale, of Kingsport.

Playing for Boys Club

Todd Foster played baseball at the Boys Club in Kingsport in 1975. He is now the assistant golf pro at Warriors Path Golf Course in Kingsport. Contributed by Freddie Foster of Kingsport.

Jump for it

Brenda Babb (No. 32), playing for Dobyns-Bennett High School, went after the jump ball during a mid-1970s basketball game against Lynn View High School in the D-B Dome. Playing with Babb was Angel Swaggerty (No. 21). Contributed by Hugh Babb of Kingsport.

New flag corps

Laura Duncan (right) and Greta Gronbeck were members of the newly revived flag corps at Dobyns-Bennett High School in 1976. Their uniforms consisted of old band uniform tops that were made shorter, skirts and patent leather boots that the girls cut the heels off of to make them easier to march in. Contributed by Laura Duncan of Rogersville.

Ozzie's ball

Rickie "Ozzie" Osborne played football at Ketron High School from 1971-74 and was the team's quarterback his junior and senior years. In addition, he played baseball and basketball, and ran track. He planned to play football at the University of Tennessee but was injured during spring practice. He now lives in Nashville. Contributed by Mildred Osborne, mother of Rickie Osborne, of Kingsport.

First game at Virginia High

On Sept. 27, 1974, the intense rivalry between Gate City High School and Virginia High School in Bristol continued. Only this time this game was the first one played at Virginia High's football field. The previous year, Virginia High had beaten Gate City on its home turf. On this night, Gate City returned the favor, clobbering Virginia High 62 to 12. Pictured are Ronnie Cato carrying the ball for Virginia High meeting defense from Dwayne Foster (No. 81), Lindy Collins (No. 41), Mickey Rogers (No. 2) and David Wolfe (No. 83). Contributed by Dwayne Foster of Kingsport.

ETSU cheerleaders

Among the members of the 1979 ETSU cheerleading squad were (front row, from left) Karen Kidd, Sandy Nelson, Carlyle Bruce, Tim Lyons, Ginger Brandon, Vicki Hodge, (second row, from left) Jean Osborne, Bob Sisk, Janet Harris, Lee Kyle, David Lilly and Susan Sisson. Contributed by Ginger Brandon of Kingsport.

Whale of a player

Keith "Whale" Gibson, shown here in 1971, played on the offensive line for Church Hill High School. He went on to play at Virginia Tech for four years on a football scholarship. Contributed by Keith Gibson.

Offense and defense

Kenneth Gibson, shown here in 1970, played offense and defense for the Church Hill High School football team. He later played at Vanderbilt University on a football scholarship. Contributed by Kenneth Gibson of Kingsport.

Going for two

Jeff Kilby, a point guard for Sullivan Central High School in 1977, helped Central beat Abingdon High School in the early rounds of the Big 6 Tournament, which also included Tennessee, Sullivan East, Virginia and John Battle high schools. Central, coached at the time by Dickie Warren, played in the finals, but Tennessee High won the tournament. Kilby played four years at Central. Contributed by Wendy Kilby of Kingsport.

Lynn View fullback

Harvey Hall played fullback for Lynn View High School in 1978. Contributed by Janet Hall of Church Hill.

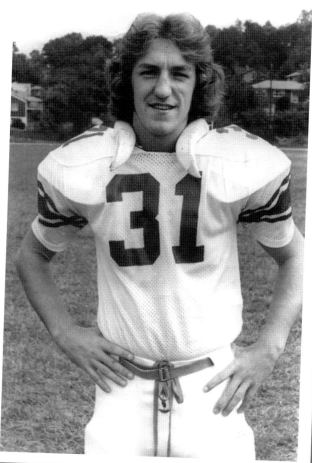

The Squaws

The Dobyns-Bennett High School girls basketball team, which in 1975-76 was still known as the Squaws, consisted of (back row, from left) Patty Miller, Janet Stiles, Cindy Adams, Angel Swaggerty, Vanessa Logan, Johnnie May Swaggerty, Brenda Babb, Maureen Danehy, Ellen (last name unknown), Tricia (last name unknown), Twinkle Bell, Elaine Watterson and Jackie Carnes. Cecilia Konyn (second row, center) was the coach. Contributed by Brenda (Babb) McCroskey of Sevierville, Tennessee.

Boar hunting

Josh Staples, Marvin Williams and Roy Depew got two boar while hunting at Tellico Plains wildlife station in the early 1970s. The photo was made at Cherokee Finance in Kingsport. Contributed by Roy Depew of Mount Carmel.

A standout

Walter "Lee" Taylor was a standout basketball player at Lynn View High School, from which he graduated in 1956. In addition, he played fast-pitch softball, at which he also was a standout; baseball and basketball. He ran track and enjoyed bowling and hunting. In 2005, he was inducted into the Kingsport Bowling Association Hall of Fame. Taylor served as an official for the Tennessee Secondary Schools Athletic Association and for the city league basketball for more than 25 years. He was the youngest official ever selected to referee the state AAA basketball tournament. He died on July 26, 2005 of cancer. Contributed by Louise Taylor of Church Hill.

Dutch Masters Open

Dennis Lane (second from left) finished third in the Professional Bowlers Association's Dutch Masters Open in 1978. Dick Ritger (second from right) won the Open. Lane and Ritger were on tour together at this time. Ritger, now an elite coach, is in the Bowling Hall of Fame. The two were honored by corporate officials from Dutch Masters (U.S. Tobacco Co.) Contributed by Dennis Lane of Kingsport.

TV finalist

In 1978, Dennis Lane was a TV finalist in the Professional Bowlers Association's national tournament held at the MGM Grand in Reno, Nevada. Lane finished fourth in that tournament. He bowled professionally for eight years and still does some senior tours. Contributed by Dennis Lane of Kingsport.

Loved fishing

Bruce Bloomer enjoyed camping, boating and fishing, but he loved fishing most. He caught this fish in Dale Hollow Lake in 1979. Contributed by Mary (Spears) Bloomer, widow of Bruce Bloomer, of Church Hill.

Future Cougars

In 1970, Jeff Holt and David Cook practiced their football moves in the Holts' back yard, getting ready for the gridiron at Sullivan Central High School, from which they graduated in 1981. Contributed by Sue Holt of Blountville.

Tennis, anyone?

Though Scott Stidham played in the VFW Little League in Church Hill in 1978, he later played tennis at Volunteer High School and was named All-Conference for two years. He also played tennis at Carson-Newman College. Contributed by Wanda Stidham of Church Hill.

First-name basis

It was easy to tell who was who on the 1979 Church Hill T-ball Maroon Team, sponsored by Acme Sports. The team members were (front row, from left) Matthew Mitchell, Eric Christian, Troy Lawson, Steve Smith, Chuck McLain, Michelle Smith, Marty Moore, (back row, from left) Joe Fleenor, Scott Barrett, Chris Burchfield, Loree Roller, Jerrilynn Greer and Jeremy Moore. Contributed by Marty Moore of Kingsport.

Cheers for Church Hill

The Church Hill High School cheerleading squad for 1970-71 consisted of (front row, from left) Denise Booker, Sherry Salley (on shoulders), Deb Marsh, Sharon Christian (deceased), Alice Sensabaugh, Shirley Jane Creasy, and Carolyn Gibbons (on shoulders). Contributed by Carolyn Gibbons of Church Hill who is now a cheerleading coach at Church Hill Middle School and Volunteer High School.

Maroon on top

The 1977 Church Hill T-ball Maroon Team, sponsored by Acme Sports, was unbeaten that season. The team members were (front row, from left) Paul Lisenby, Chris Dyer, Eric Christian, (second row, from left) Chuck McLain, Jeremy Moore, unknown, Craig Christian, Scottie Barrett, (third row, from left) Jerrilyn Greer, Paula Lisenby, Jimbo Greer, Bobby Duty, Tommy Bernard, John-John Barrett, uknown, Billy Duty, Mike Arnold, (not pictured) Chris Bright and Kim Bright. Contributed by Marty Moore of Kingsport.

All in the family

For the Joneses, softball and baseball were big pastimes in 1977. (From left) Chris Jones, 10, played baseball for the Lynn Garden Optimist team. Bill Jones played for the Mead Knights in the city industrial league, and Randy Jones, 12, played baseball for the Bell Ridge Ruritan team. Contributed by Joan Jones, wife of Bill and mother of Chris and Randy, of Kingsport.

Here's the pitch

Joey Tranbarger was a pitcher for the eighth-grade baseball team at John Sevier Junior High School in 1975-76. He later played at Dobyns-Bennett High School. Contributed by Joyce Tranbarger of Kingsport.

Knights exemplar

The Mead Knights softball team were the city industrial league champions in 1975, with a record of 23-3. The team won two and lost two in the state tournament in Murfreesboro, Tennessee. The team members were (front row, from left) Lynn Steffey, Larry Goins, Jack Parsons, Bill Jones, Cecil Carter, Charlie Fisher, (back row, from left) Bill Christian, Dwight Church, Bill Sallings, Eddie Moore (deceased), Wayne McConnell, Roy Bear, Larry Woods and (not pictured) R.B. Hartley. Contributed by Billy R. Jones of Kingsport.

Thumbs up

The Mount Carmel Elementary School basketball team was proud of its performance in February 1976. Among the team members were Steve Clark (kneeling, left) and Randall Clark (kneeling, right). Contributed by Jewel Clark of Church Hill.

Bowling belles

Mildred Sampson (left) and Mildred Smith, both of Kingsport, bowled in the doubles tournament at the 1971 Women's International Bowling Congress in Atlanta, Georgia. Contributed by Mildred Sampson of Kingsport.

School of the Empty Hand

The American School of the Empty Hand taught karate in Blountville in the early 1970s, led by trainer David Collins (front, center). Among the students were Gene Clark (standing, left), and his sons Randy and Steve Clark (front, right). Contributed by Jewel Clark of Church Hill.

Power team

The Tennessee Eastman Recreation Club's softball team (Power and Service) in 1976 consisted of (front row, from left) Phil Hoard, Leonard Salyers, Otis Debord, Jim McLain, Jack Berry, David Reece, (back row, from left) B.G. Hall, manager; John Fleenor, Jerry Moore, Wayne Salyers, James "Skip" Evans, Freddie Carter, and Woody Mounger. Contributed by Effie Berry of Jekyll Island, Georgia.

Man to man

Charlie Leonard (left) and Jack Berry played opposite each other in the Tennessee Eastman Recreation Club's basketball league in 1970. Contributed by Effie Berry of Jekyll Island, Georgia.

Optimist football

Tim Shanks, seen here in 1978, played football for both the Sullivan Optimist and the Sullivan Middle School teams. He started playing football at Sullivan South High School but broke his leg freshman year. Contributed by Tim Shanks of Fort Myers, Florida.

All-Tournament team

The 1970 District 1 All-Tournament team in basketball consisted of (front row, from left) David Hunley, Dobyns-Bennett High School; Mark Mason, most valuable player, Sullivan East High School; Mike Pyle, Sullivan East; Jerry Thompson, D-B; Mike Evans, D-B; (back row, from left) Sam Boyd, Tennessee High School; Danny Martin, Sullivan Central High School; Bob McGhee, Hampton High School; Johnny Cox, Hampton; and Mike Freeman, Sullivan High School. Contributed by Mark Mason of Piney Flats.

College play

Mark Mason (No. 22), who was a basketball standout playing guard for Sullivan East High School, signed with East Tennessee State University but then transferred to Carson-Newman College and played there for three years, including 1974. Contributed by Mark Mason of Piney Flats.

ETSU basketball

Danny Martin, who played guard at Sullivan Central High School, signed for four years of basketball at East Tennessee State University. He was redshirted one year, played for two years, including 1973, and then sat out for two years following knee surgery. Contributed by Danny Martin of Kingsport.

Hunting at Tellico Plains

Though wild boar hunting was their favorite, Brad Hoover (left) and his father, Ted, enjoyed hunting ram at Tellico Plains, Tennessee. This photo dates from 1977. Contributed by Brad Hoover of Kingsport.

Holliston Mills softball

The 1973 Holliston Mills softball team of New Canton, Tennessee, consisted of (front row, from left) Sally Parton, Mary Reynolds, Hope Barton, Diane Richardson, Brenda Strong, (second row, from left) Kathy Basket, Susie Ladd, Dot Bright, Connie Bruner, Blanche Craddock, Odie Davis, (back row, from left) Coach Richard Britton and Coach Jay Wade (deceased). Contributed by Sally Parton of Mount Carmel.

Four years of football

William "Bill" Light, seen here in 1978-79, played football at Dobyns-Bennett High School for four years. Contributed by Bill Light of Kingsport.

Boys Club baseball

Playing baseball on a team at the Kingsport Boys Club in 1970 were (front row, from left) John Doster, Paul McGill, unknown, Jerry Bradley, Jeff Sharrett, Wayne Epps, unknown, (back row, from left) Lewis Justis, unknown, Billy Cross, Bob McCall, Wayne Swann, David McGill and Bobby Lane. They were coached by Joey Bowen (back, left), assistant; and Haywood Bowen. The former Boys Club building is seen in the background. Contributed by Keith Justis of Kingsport.

East Hawkins league

Bobby Wines Jr., played baseball for the East Hawkins County League in 1977. Contributed by Sally Parton, mother of Bobby Wines Jr., of Mount Carmel.

Three years undefeated

Ronnie Horton (front row, from left), Steve Jones, Michael Leeper (back row, from left), Arthur Bradley and Greg Hickman were the five starters on the John Sevier Junior High School basketball team in seventh, eighth and ninth grades. The team, seen here in 1975, was undefeated all three years. All four played basketball, at least for a time, at Dobyns-Bennett High School. Leeper, Bradley and Hickman play for four years at D-B. Horton and Jones played for two years, and then played football and ran track. Contributed by Ronnie C. Horton of Kingsport.

Fastest man

Ronnie Horton (second from left) won the 100-yard dash in his freshman year in 1976 at Dobyns-Bennett High School. He ran against (from left) Clark Duncan, Erwin High School; Van Williams, Science Hill High School; Tommy Henry, D-B; and an unknown runner from Morristown. Contributed by Ronnie C. Horton of Kingsport.

RNR basketball

Keith Justis played basketball as a ninth-grader at Ross N. Robinson Junior High School in 1979. On Little League teams, he played with Randy Harkleroad, Bruce Tranbarger and Rodney Blye. Contributed by Danny Justis, father of Keith Justis, of Kingsport.

Hurdlers relay team

Coach Tom Coughenour (third from right) trained the high hurdles relay team at Dobyns-Bennett High School, which in 1978 included Kenneth "Scat" Springs (second from left) and Ronnie Horton (right). Contributed by Elise Horton, wife of Ronnie Horton, of Kingsport.

Little Gators

The Kingsport Boys Club Gators flag football team, made up of 5- to 7-year-olds in 1970, consisted of (front row, from left) Doug Byington, unknown, Tim Burke, Bill Robinson, Mike Horn, Alex Carlin, Robbie Stepp, Tim Stepp, Steve Reed, (second row, from left) Dale Larkins, Bobby Bishop, Todd Oaks, Mark Bacon, John Byington, Gary Gause, Lee Austin and Chris DeGreen. The team was coached by Coach Stepp and Coach Gause. Contributed by Sandra Byington of Kingsport.

D-B wrestler

Tony Stamper wrestled at Dobyns-Bennett High School during his junior year, 1978-79. He was coached by Tony England. Contributed by Dottie Keel of Kingsport.

Touchdown return

In 1979, during an East Tennessee State University football game versus Middle Tennessee State University at MTSU, Ronnie C. Horton (carrying ball) set a school record for the longest touchdown kickoff return running 103 yards, though the record indicates the run was 100 yards. Horton also holds the school record at Dobyns-Bennett High School for a football interception returned for a touchdown -- 100 yards -- set in 1978. Contributed by Elise Horton, wife of Ronnie Horton, of Kingsport.

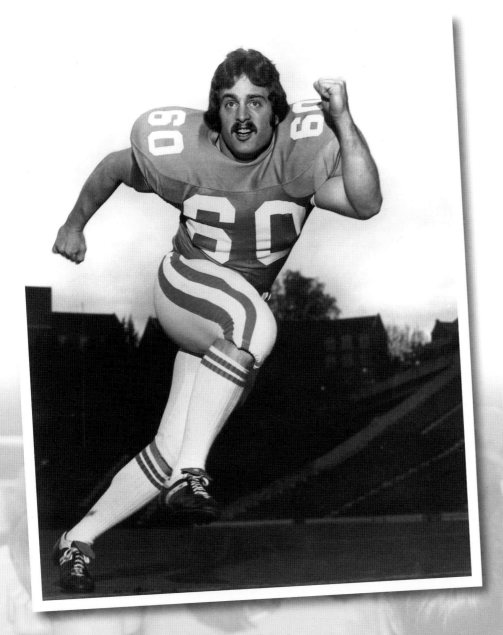

All everything

Steve White, who played football at Dobyns-Bennett High School, was named All Big 9 (1971, 1972), Knoxville Journal All East Tennessee (1972) and Knoxville Journal All State (1972). He graduated from D-B in 1973 and played football at the University of Tennessee, from which he earned a degree in business administration in 1978. He now holds a first-degree black belt in Choon Sil Taekwondo. From 1997-1999, he was assistant coach for the Harpeth High School boys soccer team in Kingston Springs, Tenneessee. He was named head coach in 2000 and coached until 2003. He lives with his family in Antioch, Tennessee. Contributed by Vivian C. White of Kingsport.

Autograph racquet

In honor of his winning the national racquetball championship in 1977, Wilson Sporting Goods Co., designed the Davey Bledsoe Autograph racquet. Bledsoe, a native of Kingsport, took up racquetball in 1972. He won the National Intercollegiate Singles Championships in 1973, while a student at the University of Tennessee. He turned professional in 1975 and won the National Doubles Championship that year. In addition to winning the 1977 National Racquetball Club National Indoor Championship in San Diego, California, he won the 1978 National Outdoor Championship. Contributed by Nikki Brooks, sister of Davey Bledsoe, of Kingsport.

Senior Devils

The seniors on the Gate City High School football team in 1976 were (front row, from left) Chuck Willis, Rick Frazier, Keener Fry, Richard Jones, Tim Blankenbeckler, Lindy Collins, (back row, from left) Rick Shoemaker, Johnny Redwine, Lynn Elliott, Lester Bledsoe, Tim Wells, Rick Ervin and Tim Poston. Contributed by Frankie Collins, mother of Lindy Collins, of Weber City, Virginia.

Pee Wee football

John "Joco" Crawford played Pee Wee football at the Kingsport Boys Club under Coach Eddie Durham in the mid-1970s. Contributed by Jane Crawford of Kingsport.

Basketball 'Blazers

The 1974-75 Daniel Boone High School Trailblazers basketball team consisted of (front row, from left) Victor Tucker, Mark Halvorsen, David Ray, Greg Kilday, Greg Barnett, Ronnie Massengill, Jeff Hilton, (back row, from left) Coach Clarence Mabe, Joel Coggins, Kent Keebler, Benny Snyder, Mark Mears, Andy Barnes, Eugene Shaw and Coach Bobby Snyder. Coach Snyder was Boone's first coach and his tenure extended a number of years. Contributed Dorothy Mears, mother of Mark Mears, of Kingsport.

Going for the win

Richard Stidham played guard for the Church Hill Middle School basketball team in 1979-80, which had an overall win-loss record of 12-3. The team was unbeaten in its conference, 6-0. Stidham also played at Volunteer High School. Contributed by Wanda Stidham, mother of Richard Stidham, of Church Hill.

All-State senior

Jeff Duncan played running back for the Ketron High School football team all four years of his high school career, and was named All-State his senior year in 1976. Contributed by Jeff Duncan of Blountville.

Sweet victory

Ketron and Church Hill high schools had a huge rivalry in the 1970s, and in the fall of 1974 that rivalry was increased by the teams' state ranking, with Church Hill in fourth, and Ketron at fifth. In this game, which featured Jeff Duncan (right) catching a pass for Ketron against Church Hill defender Dean Way, Ketron beat Church Hill. Contributed by Jeff Duncan of Blountville.

Golf champion

In 1975, Jim Cooper played in one of his many Greater Kingsport Amateur golf tournaments. Cooper started playing golf at age 9 at Silver Lake Golf Course in Church Hill. He later played at Vanderbilt University and the University of North Carolina. He's a GKA champion and has won the Silver Lake Open Championships six times, the Ridgefields Club Championships two times and the Silver Lake Club Championships eight times. He has won twenty-four individual tournaments, not counting club championships. Contributed by Sydney Cooper of Kingsport.

Fourth-grade football

In 1977, when John Morelock was in fourth grade, he played football for the Optimist Club at Sullivan West Elementary School. Contributed by Carol Roller, sister of John Morelock, of Gate City, Virginia.

Optimist Club football

In 1977, when Henry Morelock was in third grade, he played football for the Optimist Club at Sullivan West Elementary School. Contributed by Carol Roller, sister of Henry Morelock, of Gate City, Virginia.

Defensive tackle

Michael Lane, seen here in 1978-79, started playing football in grade school and played all four years he was at Ketron High School, where he was a defensive tackle. Contributed by Barbara K. Lane, mother of Michael Lane, of Kingsport.

First girl

Lori Ferguson (second row, second from left) was the first girl to play in the Bloomingdale Little League. Her teammates on the 1979 Pirates team, sponsored by Bloomingdale Ruritan Club, were (front row, from left) Michael Depew (deceased), Jonathan Depew, Brian Hawn, Tony Lapomia, unknown, unknown, (second row, from left) Terry Doran, Ferguson, Mark Ferguson, unknown. The coaches were Doug Ferguson (back, left), and Paul McGhee. Contributed by Don Depew of Kingsport.

AAU basketball

In 1973, a group of recently graduated high school basketball players formed a team, sponsored by Acme Sports, to play in the Southeastern American Amateur Union tournament in Birmingham, Alabama. The team beat the Tuscaloosa, Alabama, team 121-115 in its first game, but had to play its second game just six hours later against Montgomery, Alabama. The team lost 96-94. However, the Acme team won the consolation game against Tullahoma, Tennessee, placing third. Two of the team's players, Marcus Osborne and Mark Mason, made the all-tournament squad. The other team members were Woody Mounger, Larry Lawson, Tommy Thompson, Ted Rafalowski, Tom Rafalowski, Sherman Johnson and Doug Wagner. Arthel Salyer coached the team. Contributed by Woody Mounger of Kingsport.

Cheering for Bears

The cheerleaders for the Bears Pee Wee League football team in 1971 were (front row, from left) Missy Gilreath, Robin Anderson, Robin Russell, Amy Gilreath, Becky Reed, (back row, from left) Tina Evans, Patty Salley, Susie Courtney, Lisa Christian, Kennetha Conant, Sonya Russell and Linda Chapell. The photo was taken at what was then the Church Hill High School football field. It is now the Church Hill Middle School football field. Contributed by Carol Gilreath, mother of Missy and Amy Gilreath, of Church Hill.

Basketball scholarship

After playing four years of basketball at Lynn View High School, graduating in 1976, Tim Dean (No. 32) won a basketball scholarship to play at King College in Bristol, Tennessee. More than 25 years later, he served on the Kingsport Board of Education. He now works for GlaxoSmithKline, and he and his wife, Lisa, have two sons, Tyler and Matthew, who played football at Dobyns-Bennett High School. Contributed by Bob Dean of Kingsport.

Trumpet talent

Amy Gilreath (front, center) began playing trumpet in seventh grade and played throughout her high school years at Church Hill High School, and participated in the Rogersville Christmas Parade in 1979. She received a bachelor's degree from Eastern Kentucky University at Richmond, and received a master's degree and a doctorate in trumpet performance from the University of Illinois. She is now a professor of trumpet at Illinois State University and principal trumpet in the Peoria Sympony and the Illinois Symphony at Springfield. She also teaches brass/trumpet in Orveitta, Italy. Contributed by Thomas Gilreath of Church Hill.

Lynn Garden cheerleaders

Cheryl Kiser (standing, left) and Tammy Wilson (standing, right) were Lynn Garden Elementary School cheerleaders in 1971-72. Contributed by David Kilgore, friends of Cheryl Kiser and Tammy Wilson who cheered for the basketball team David played on, of Kingsport.

At the ready

Diane Depew Melton, seen here in 1971-72, was a majorette at Sullivan High School for four years. Contributed by Shirley Depew of Kingsport.

Rock Springs cheerleaders

The Rock Springs Elementary School Mustangs cheerleaders in 1974 were (front row, from left) Betty Quillen, Tammy Carroll, (second row, from left) Ladonna Selby, Jennifer Light, Becky Greer, Susan Snavely, Kay Barrett, (back row, from left) Nancy Lady and Qwana Wickline. The seventh- and eighth-graders cheered for the basketball team at the old Rock Springs Elementary School, which was on Rock Springs Road. Contributed by Annett Barrett Christian of Kingsport.

Successful partnership

Norman Lipe and Richard Gray played doubles tennis together for 10 years and won 20 trophies, including first place in the Morristown Tennis Tournament in 1975 at the Frank Lorino Park. They also won the "B" Kingsport Open Tennis Tournament in 1979. Gray played tennis in college and was No. 1 on Lincoln Memorial University's tennis team. Lipe took up tennis as a hobby. He was inducted into the Hawkins County Tennis Association Hall of Fame and the Rogersville Parks and Recreation Hall of Fame. Contributed by Norman Lipe of Rogersville.

Loving football

Chad McLain was all smiles playing football for the Kingsport Boys Club in 1979. Contributed by Sue McLain of Church Hill.

Jumping high

Brenda Babb of Dobyns-Bennett High School jumped five feet, three and a half inches to win the girls' high jump at the Knoxville News-Sentinel Relays on April 1, 1978. Contributed by Hugh Babb of Kingsport.

Dallas Cowboys Junior

The Dallas Cowboys Pee Wee League team competed in 1971 and included No. 29 Harold Wayne McMillian (deceased).
Contributed by Billy R. McMillian of Kingsport.

Queen for a day

Sally Russin was crowned homecoming queen at Sullivan Central High School in November 1971. Contributed by Mark Dingus, husband of Sally Russin Dingus, of Blountville.

On the ball

One of the Kingsport Boys Club basketball teams in 1970 consisted of (front row, from left) Colin Smith, David Thompson, Frank Kiser (deceased), Alan Jones, (second row, from left) Flint Gray, Mike Reynolds, Brad Hoover and Scott Jennings. The coaches were O.K. Roberts (left) and Ted Hoover. Contributed by Brad Hoover, son of Ted Hoover, of Kingsport.

Family affair

Lamarr Stout (left) and Jim Stout played on a baseball team at the Kingsport Boys Club and liked having their sister, Rebecca Stout, cheer them on. The children's father, Dorman L. Stout, was a baseball coach at the Boys Club. Contributed by Mary Ann Stout of Kingsport.

On track

Mark Dingus (left) and Don Carter spent some time warming up for a local track meet in 1978. The two were students at the University of Tennessee at Chattanooga. Dingus has been the cross-country coach at Sullivan Central High School for 18 years. Contributed by Mollie Dingus of Kingsport.

Parade of champions

The Eagles were the 1970 Blountville Little League champions and were honored with a ride in the Blountville Fourth of July Parade. The team members were (clockwise from far left) Hasque Delp, Mike Glover, Larry Hughes, Larry Beverly, Terry Jones, Mitch Moore, Sammy Sanders, P.W. Smith, Scotty Webb, Rusty Stewart, unknown, Mickey Jones, bat boy; David Webb, unknown, Mike Pullon and Danny Leonard. Terry Jones was wearing sunglasses not because the day was particularly bright but because he had been stung by a bee. Contributed by Michael Glover of Blountville.

Twin players

Twin brothers Donnie and Ronnie Godsey played baseball for the Jaycees Little League team in Gate City, Virginia, in 1970. When they were older, they made the All-Star team, following in the footsteps of their four older brothers. Contributed by Nancy Godsey of Gate City.

Mommy cheerleaders

The mothers of the Gate City High School football team players shocked the student body by leading cheers during a 1974 pep rally much to the delight of long-time legendary coach Harry Fry (on stage). The moms were Mrs. Cornett, Mrs. Humphries, Mrs. Foster, Mrs. Begley, Mrs. Seaver and Mrs. Frazier. Contributed by Dwayne Foster, son of Shirley Foster, of Kingsport.

East All-Stars

Some of the local members of the Tennessee Secondary Schools Athletic Association's East All-Star Team, who beat the West team 28-14 in the East-West All-Star game of 1976 in Murfreesboro, were Bob Johnson (No. 84) and Chuck Cole (No. 50) of Church Hill High School; Joey Holt (No. 13) of Sullivan Central High School; and Linc Jarvis (No. 80) and Doug Whetsel (No. 63) of Dobyns-Bennett High School. Whetsel was named the most valuable player of the game. Contributed by Jack Jarvis of Kingsport.

Fast pitch

Carl Sandidge (deceased) played fast-pitch softball with the Kingsport city league softball team sponsored by Smith's Plumbing, including this game in June 1971. The team won several games and traveled to tournaments in Chattanooga and California. He is now deceased. Contributed by Betty Jean Sandidge of Surgoinsville.

Bats ready

In June 1975, David Jones, then 12, had his bats ready to play ball with his Civitan Little League baseball team. They played ball at what is now Grogan Park in Gate City, Virginia. Contributed by Janice Jones, mother of David Jones, of Gate City, Virginia.

Sevier shortstop

Lamarr Stout played shortstop for the John Sevier Junior High School junior varsity baseball team in 1974. Contributed by Mary Ann Stout of Kingsport.

Brothers at play

Lamarr (left) and Jim Stout played football at the Kingsport Boys Club and were coached by their father Dorman L. Stout. Contributed by Lamarr Stout of Kingsport.

Cheers for Blountville

The Blountville Elementary School cheerleaders in 1978-79 were (front) Tuesday Arwood, (second row, from left) Ann Marie Almaroad, Rhonda Boyd, Amy Carter, Vickie McNamara, (back row, from left) Michele Dixon, Connie Lindamood, Rhnea Shaffer, Lori Dishner and Leslie Weaver. Contributed by Lori Dishner Hillman of Charlotte, North Carolina.

Boys will play

One of the Kingsport Boys Club baseball teams in 1972 consisted of (front row, from left) Kenneth Hendrix, Lamarr Stout, Kenneth "Rocky" Maloy, Drew Ring, Walter Holland, (second row, from left) Pat Breeding, Chuck Pecktol, Bowen Scott, Vic Ring, Steve Pecktol, (back row, from left) Assistant Coach Flem Pecktol, Jim Stout, Ward Carter, Clark "Guts" Carter, Mark Rosenbaum and Coach Dorman Stout. Contributed by Jim Stout of Kingsport.

Sullivan West majorettes

The majorettes for Sullivan West High School in 1978 were (from right) Penny Hood, Sandi Williams Chaddock, Carla Powell and unknown. Chaddock was a majorette for four years and played clarinet and drums in the band. She graduated in 1980. Contributed by George and Edna Williams of Kingsport.

Bucs basketball

The Sullivan High School Pirates basketball team in 1973-74 consisted of (standing, from left) Tommy Stice, Don Teague, Steve Cox, Randy Blakely, Mark Conkin, Robert Littleton, Harry Hamblen, Mike Williams, Terry Hudson, Dave Light, Bo Ryans and Randy Holland. Carl Childress (front) was the coach. Contributed by George and Edna Williams of Kingsport.

The Phantom

"Phantom" Phil Rogers played football and baseball for Gate City High School all four years he was there, including 1970. He was part of the famous, athletic Rogers family, which also included brothers Anthony, Stan and Mickey. Contributed by Brent Roberts of Gate City, Virginia.

West quarterback

Gary Wayne Shanks was quarterback for the Sullivan West High School football team in 1972-73. He also played baseball for the school and held records in that sport. Both sports were good training for his career as a football and baseball coach at Sullivan Middle School. Shanks also has coached basketball at Sullivan Middle and freshman baseball at Sullivan South High School. Contributed by Pauline Shanks of Kingsport.

Central guard

Danny Martin (No. 20) played guard for the Sullivan Central High School basketball team in 1970. At that time, the team playing at home wore even-numbered jerseys, while the away team wore odd-numbered jerseys. Martin later signed to play basketball at East Tennessee State University. Contributed by Danny Martin of Kingsport.

Kodel Fibers team

Bill Long was the pitcher for the Kodel Fibers softball team in the Eastman Recreation League in 1974. Contributed by Bill Long of Kingsport.

Pirates beat all

The Pirates Pee Wee Reese team were the city champions with a 9-0 record in 1975. The team members were (front row, from left) Gary Smith, Roger Sutherland, (second row, from left) Hunter Kitchens, Tommy Smith, Keith Justis, Trey Kistner, (third row, from left) Tommy Thomas, Richard Scheer, David Clark and Earl Feathers. Coach Bob Akers (back) coached Little League for several years in Kingsport. He now often works football games at Dobyns-Bennett High School. Contributed by Danny Justis of Kingsport.

Playing trombone

Dwane Dishner played trombone for four years, including 1977, in the Sullivan Central High School Band. Contributed by Dwane Dishner of Knoxville.

Enjoyable evenings

Many enjoyable evenings were spent watching the Civitan Little League baseball team in June 1975. The team played at the Gate City Little League field, now Grogan Park. The team members were (front row, from left) Eric McMurray, Billy Kendrick, David Quillen, Jimmy Meade, Richard Depew, Johnny Kendrick, Mark McDavid, (second row, from left) Eddie Barger (deceased), Glen Heffner, Mark Sampson, David Jones, Micky Carter, Steve McClellan and Clay Pendleton. The coaches were Carl Barger (back, left) and Bill Carter. Contributed by Janice Jones, mother of David Jones, of Gate City, Virginia.